THIS BOOK

BELONGS TO

....

....

Thank you for Purchasing my book and taking the time to read it from front to back. I am always grateful when a reader chooses my work and I hope you enjoyed it!

With the vast selection available online, I am touched that you chose to be purchasing my work and take valuable time out of your life to read it. My hope is that you feel you made the right decision.

I very much would like to know what you thought of the book. Please take the time to write an honest and informative review on Amazon.com. Your experience and opinions will be of great benefit to me and those readers looking to make an informed choice.

With much thanks.

Table of Contents

Crocheting for babies is a popular choice among crafters and parents alike for several reasons. Firstly, crochet items for babies are not only adorable but also practical. From cozy blankets and hats to cute booties and stuffed animals, crocheted baby items are not only visually appealing but also serve a functional purpose. These handmade items can keep babies warm and comfortable, especially during the colder months.

Secondly, crocheting for babies allows for customization and personalization. When you crochet a baby item, you have the freedom to choose the colors, patterns, and designs that you prefer. This means that you can create unique and one-of-a-kind pieces that reflect your own style and taste. Additionally, you can also personalize these items by adding the baby's name or initials, making them even more special and meaningful.

Furthermore, crocheting for babies can be a rewarding and fulfilling experience. The process of creating something with your own hands can be incredibly satisfying, and seeing the end result of your hard work can bring a sense of accomplishment. Crocheting for babies also allows you to express your creativity and imagination, as you can experiment with different stitches, techniques, and yarns to create beautiful and intricate designs.

In addition to the personal satisfaction, crocheting for babies can also be a thoughtful and heartfelt gift. Handmade baby items are often cherished and treasured by both parents and babies. They can become heirlooms that are passed down through generations, creating a lasting connection and memory. Giving a crocheted baby item as a gift shows that you have put time, effort, and love into creating something special for the little one.

Lastly, crocheting for babies can be a practical and cost-effective option. Buying baby items from stores can be expensive, especially when considering the frequency at which babies outgrow their clothes and accessories. By crocheting baby items yourself, you can save money while still providing high-quality and unique pieces for your little one or as gifts for others.

In conclusion, crocheting for babies offers a multitude of benefits. From the practicality and customization to the personal satisfaction and cost-effectiveness, crocheting baby items allows for creativity, personalization, and the creation of cherished keepsakes. Whether you are a seasoned crocheter or a beginner, crocheting for babies can be a rewarding and enjoyable experience.

Sentimental value refers to the emotional significance or attachment that an object, person, or experience holds for an individual. It is a subjective and personal perception that goes beyond the material or practical worth of something. Sentimental value is often associated with cherished memories, sentimental objects, or sentimental experiences that evoke strong emotions, nostalgia, or a sense of connection.

When something has sentimental value, it means that it holds a special place in someone's heart and has a deeper meaning beyond its physical attributes. It could be an item that has been passed down through generations, such as a family heirloom or a piece of jewelry. These objects carry the memories and stories of those who came before, making them precious and irreplaceable.

Sentimental value can also be attached to experiences or places that hold significant memories. For example, a childhood home or a favorite vacation spot may hold sentimental value because of the memories and emotions associated with them. These places become a symbol of comfort, happiness, or a sense of belonging.

Sentimental value is deeply personal and can vary from person to person. What may hold sentimental value for one individual may not have the same significance for another. It is often influenced by personal history, cultural background, and individual experiences. For instance, a handwritten letter from a loved one may hold sentimental value for someone who values personal connections and meaningful gestures, while it may not hold the same significance for someone who places more importance on material possessions.

The sentimental value of an object or experience can also evolve over time. As life circumstances change, certain things may gain or lose sentimental value. For example, a piece of jewelry that was once a symbol of love and commitment in a relationship may become a painful reminder after a breakup. Similarly, an object that was once associated with a negative experience may gain sentimental value as time passes and the emotions attached to it change.

Sentimental value can bring comfort, joy, and a sense of identity to individuals. It allows them to connect with their past, their loved ones, and their own emotions. It can also serve as a reminder of what is truly important in life, beyond material possessions. Sentimental value is a powerful force that can shape our relationships, our choices, and our overall well-being.

Handmade quality refers to the level of craftsmanship and attention to detail that goes into creating a product by hand. It is a term often used to describe items that are made by skilled artisans using traditional techniques and tools, rather than being mass-produced by machines.

When something is described as having handmade quality, it implies that it has been carefully crafted with care and precision. Each step of the production process is carried out by hand, allowing for a greater level of control and customization. This attention to detail results in a product that is unique and of higher quality than those produced on a large scale.

One of the key advantages of handmade quality is the ability to create products that are tailored to individual needs and preferences. Artisans can work closely with customers to understand their specific requirements and create a product that meets their exact specifications. This level of customization is often not possible with mass-produced items, which are designed to appeal to a broad market.

Handmade quality also often goes hand in hand with the use of high-quality materials. Artisans who create products by hand typically have a deep understanding of the materials they work with and select only the best for their creations. This ensures that the final product is not only visually appealing but also durable and long-lasting.

Furthermore, handmade quality often carries with it a sense of authenticity and uniqueness. Each item is a one-of-a-kind creation, reflecting the skill and creativity of the artisan who made it. This stands in contrast to mass-produced items, which are often identical and lack the personal touch that comes with handmade craftsmanship.

In addition to the aesthetic and functional benefits, supporting handmade quality also has social and environmental advantages. By purchasing handmade products, consumers are supporting local artisans and small businesses, helping to sustain traditional crafts and skills. Furthermore, handmade production methods often have a lower environmental impact compared to mass production, as they typically involve less energy consumption and waste generation.

In conclusion, handmade quality represents the pinnacle of craftsmanship and attention to detail. It offers a level of customization, authenticity, and uniqueness that is often lacking in mass-produced items. By choosing handmade products, consumers not only acquire a high-quality item but also support local artisans and contribute to a more sustainable and socially responsible economy.

The target audience refers to the specific group of individuals or customers that a product, service, or message is intended to reach and resonate with. Identifying and understanding the target audience is crucial for any business or organization as it helps in tailoring marketing strategies, creating relevant content, and delivering effective communication.

To determine the target audience, various factors need to be considered, such as demographics, psychographics, behavior patterns, and preferences. Demographics include characteristics such as age, gender, income level, education, occupation, and geographic location. Psychographics delve deeper into the target audience's personality traits, values, attitudes, interests, and lifestyles. Behavior patterns encompass the target audience's purchasing habits, brand loyalty, online behavior, and media consumption.

By analyzing these factors, businesses can create detailed buyer personas or customer profiles that represent their ideal target audience. These personas help in understanding the target audience's motivations, needs, pain points, and aspirations. This knowledge enables businesses to develop products and services that cater to their target audience's specific requirements and desires.

Understanding the target audience also helps in crafting effective marketing messages and communication strategies. By knowing the target audience's language, communication channels, and preferred content formats, businesses can create compelling and relevant content that resonates with their audience. This can include social media posts, blog articles, videos, podcasts, or even traditional advertising mediums such as television or print.

Moreover, identifying the target audience allows businesses to allocate their marketing resources efficiently. Instead of adopting a one-size-fits-all approach, businesses can focus their efforts on reaching the specific group of individuals who are most likely to be interested in their offerings. This targeted approach not only saves time and money but also increases the chances of generating higher conversion rates and customer engagement.

In conclusion, understanding the target audience is essential for any business or organization. It helps in tailoring marketing strategies, creating relevant content, and delivering effective communication. By analyzing demographics, psychographics, behavior patterns, and preferences, businesses can develop detailed buyer personas that represent their ideal customers. This knowledge enables businesses to create products and services that cater to their target audience's specific needs and desires. Additionally, understanding the target audience allows businesses to allocate their marketing resources efficiently and increase the chances of generating higher conversion rates and customer engagement.

A comprehensive list of all the necessary materials and tools required for a specific task or project.

When it comes to selecting yarn and hooks for your crochet projects, there are several factors to consider. Yarn and hooks play a crucial role in determining the final outcome of your project, so it's important to choose them wisely.

Firstly, let's talk about yarn. Yarn comes in various materials, weights, and textures, each with its own unique characteristics. The material of the yarn can range from natural fibers like cotton, wool, and silk to synthetic fibers like acrylic and nylon. Each material has its own advantages and disadvantages. Natural fibers tend to be more breathable and have a luxurious feel, but they may require special care and can be more expensive. On the other hand, synthetic fibers are often more affordable, easy to care for, and come in a wide range of vibrant colors.

The weight of the yarn refers to its thickness, which can vary from super fine to super bulky. The weight of the yarn you choose will depend on the type of project you're working on. For delicate and intricate projects like lacework or amigurumi, a finer weight yarn would be more suitable. For projects that require warmth and thickness, such as blankets or scarves, a heavier weight yarn would be ideal.

Texture is another important aspect to consider when selecting yarn. Yarn can be smooth, fluffy, or textured, and this can greatly impact the overall look and feel of your project. Smooth yarn is great for showcasing stitch definition and creating clean lines, while fluffy or textured yarn can add depth and interest to your work.

Now let's move on to hooks. Crochet hooks come in different sizes, which are denoted by letters or numbers. The size of the hook you choose will depend on the weight of the yarn you're using and the desired tension of your stitches. A smaller hook is typically used with finer weight yarns, while a larger hook is used with bulkier yarns. It's important to match the hook size to the yarn weight to ensure that your stitches are even and consistent.

The material of the hook is also worth considering. Crochet hooks can be made from various materials such as aluminum, plastic, wood, or even bamboo. Each material has its own unique feel and grip, so it's a matter of personal preference. Some crocheters prefer the smoothness of aluminum hooks, while others enjoy the warmth and natural feel of wooden hooks.

In conclusion, selecting the right yarn and hooks for your crochet projects is essential for achieving the desired outcome.

Gauge and tension are two important factors that play a crucial role in various industries and applications. They are used to measure and control the pressure, force, or stress exerted on a material or system.

Gauge refers to the measurement of pressure, force, or stress. It can be in the form of a physical instrument or a digital display. Gauges are commonly used in industries such as manufacturing, automotive, aerospace, and oil and gas. They are used to monitor and control the pressure in systems such as pipelines, hydraulic systems, and pneumatic systems. Gauges can also be used to measure the force exerted on materials during testing or manufacturing processes.

Tension, on the other hand, refers to the force exerted on a material or system. It is commonly used in applications such as load testing, material strength testing, and structural analysis. Tension can be measured using various instruments such as load cells, strain gauges, and tension meters. These instruments are used to measure the force exerted on a material or system and provide valuable data for analysis and control.

The relationship between gauge and tension is closely linked. The gauge is used to measure the tension or force exerted on a material or system. By measuring the tension, engineers and technicians can determine the stress levels and ensure that they are within safe limits. This is crucial in industries where the failure of a material or system can have serious consequences.

In addition to measuring tension, gauges can also be used to control tension. For example, in the textile industry, tension gauges are used to ensure that the fabric is properly tensioned during the weaving or knitting process. This helps to produce high-quality fabrics with consistent properties.

Furthermore, gauges and tension are also important in the field of metrology. Metrology is the science of measurement and plays a crucial role in ensuring the accuracy and reliability of measurements. Gauges are used to calibrate and verify the accuracy of other measuring instruments. Tension is also measured and controlled in metrology to ensure that the correct amount of force is applied during measurements.

In conclusion, gauge and tension are important factors in various industries and applications. They are used to measure and control the pressure, force, or stress exerted on a material or system. Gauges are used to measure tension and can also be used to control tension. The relationship between gauge and tension is closely linked and plays a crucial role in ensuring the safety, quality, and accuracy of measurements and processes.

Chain stitch is a type of embroidery stitch that is commonly used in hand embroidery and sewing. It is a simple and versatile stitch that can be used to create a variety of decorative patterns and designs. The stitch is formed by creating a series of loops that are connected together, resembling a chain.

To create a chain stitch, start by bringing the needle up through the fabric at the desired starting point. Then, insert the needle back into the fabric at a short distance from the starting point, creating a small loop. Before pulling the needle all the way through, pass the thread through the loop, creating a chain-like effect. Repeat this process to create a chain of stitches.

Chain stitch can be used to outline shapes, fill in areas, or create intricate patterns. It is commonly used in embroidery projects such as floral designs, lettering, and decorative borders. The stitch can be worked in a straight line or curved to follow the shape of the design.

One of the advantages of chain stitch is its flexibility. It can be easily adjusted to create different effects by varying the length and tension of the stitches. By making longer stitches, you can create a looser and more open chain, while shorter stitches will result in a tighter and more compact chain. This allows for a wide range of textures and densities in the finished embroidery.

Chain stitch can be worked with a variety of threads, including embroidery floss, pearl cotton, and even metallic threads for added sparkle. The choice of thread will depend on the desired effect and the type of fabric being used. Thicker threads will create a bolder and more pronounced chain, while finer threads will result in a delicate and intricate chain.

In addition to its decorative uses, chain stitch can also be used for practical purposes in sewing. It can be used to create strong and secure seams, as well as to attach trims and embellishments to garments and accessories.

Overall, chain stitch is a versatile and popular embroidery stitch that can be used to add texture, dimension, and visual interest to a wide range of projects. Whether you are a beginner or an experienced embroiderer, mastering the chain stitch will open up a world of creative possibilities.

Single crochet is a basic stitch in crochet that creates a tight and dense fabric. It is commonly abbreviated as sc in crochet patterns. To work a single crochet stitch, you will need a crochet hook and yarn.

To begin, make a slip knot and place it on your crochet hook. Insert the hook into the next stitch or chain space, from front to back. Yarn over (wrap the yarn around the hook) and pull it through the stitch, so that you have two loops on your hook.

Yarn over again and pull the yarn through both loops on the hook. This completes one single crochet stitch. Continue working single crochet stitches in each stitch or chain space across the row.

When you reach the end of the row, chain one to create a turning chain. This turning chain helps to maintain the height of the stitches and allows you to turn your work. Turn your work and begin the next row by inserting your hook into the first stitch or chain space.

Single crochet stitches can be used to create a variety of crochet projects, such as scarves, hats, blankets, and more. The tight and dense nature of the stitch makes it ideal for projects that require durability and structure.

In addition to working single crochet stitches in rows, you can also work them in rounds to create circular or tubular projects. To work in rounds, you will need to join each round with a slip stitch and then begin the next round in the first stitch of the previous round.

Overall, single crochet is a versatile and essential stitch in crochet. It is relatively easy to learn and can be used in a wide range of projects. Whether you are a beginner or an experienced crocheter, mastering the single crochet stitch will open up a world of possibilities for your crochet creations.

Newborn hats are essential accessories for newborn babies. These hats are specifically designed to provide warmth and comfort to the delicate heads of newborns. They are made from soft and breathable materials, such as cotton or knit fabric, to ensure that the baby's head remains cozy without causing any discomfort or irritation.

Newborn hats come in a variety of styles, colors, and patterns, allowing parents to choose the perfect hat to match their baby's outfit or personal style. Some hats feature adorable designs, such as animal ears or pom-poms, adding a touch of cuteness to the baby's overall look. Others may have adjustable straps or ties to ensure a secure fit, preventing the hat from slipping off the baby's head.

Aside from providing warmth, newborn hats also serve a practical purpose. They help regulate the baby's body temperature by preventing heat loss through the head, which is known to be a significant source of heat loss in newborns. This is especially important during the colder months or in air-conditioned environments, where babies are more susceptible to feeling cold.

Moreover, newborn hats offer protection for the baby's sensitive scalp and fontanelles. The fontanelles, also known as the soft spots on a baby's head, are areas where the skull bones have not yet fully fused together. These areas are vulnerable and require extra care and protection. Newborn hats provide a cushioning layer that helps protect the fontanelles from accidental bumps or injuries.

Newborn hats are not only practical but also make for adorable photo props. Many parents love to capture precious moments of their newborns wearing cute hats, creating lasting memories. These hats can be used during newborn photoshoots or simply for capturing everyday moments at home.

In conclusion, newborn hats are essential accessories that provide warmth, comfort, and protection for newborn babies. They come in various styles and designs, allowing parents to choose the perfect hat for their baby's needs and personal style. Whether it's for keeping the baby warm, regulating body temperature, or adding a touch of cuteness to their outfit, newborn hats are a must-have item for every newborn's wardrobe.

Baby booties are a type of footwear specifically designed for infants and young children. They are typically made from soft and comfortable materials such as cotton or fleece to ensure the utmost comfort for the baby's delicate feet. Baby booties are an essential item for parents as they provide warmth and protection to the baby's feet, especially during colder months.

These booties come in various styles and designs, ranging from simple and plain to more elaborate and decorative options. Some baby booties feature cute and playful designs such as animal faces or cartoon characters, adding an element of fun to the baby's outfit. Others may have additional features like Velcro straps or elastic bands to ensure a secure fit and easy on/off access.

The primary purpose of baby booties is to keep the baby's feet warm and cozy. Infants have a limited ability to regulate their body temperature, and their extremities, such as their feet, can get cold easily. Baby booties provide an extra layer of insulation, preventing heat loss and ensuring that the baby's feet stay warm and comfortable.

In addition to providing warmth, baby booties also offer protection to the baby's feet. As infants start to explore their surroundings and learn to crawl or walk, their feet are exposed to various surfaces and potential hazards. Baby booties act as a barrier, shielding the baby's feet from rough or uneven surfaces, sharp objects, and other potential dangers.

Furthermore, baby booties can also help with the development of the baby's feet. They provide a certain level of support and stability, which can aid in the proper alignment of the baby's feet and ankles. This is particularly important as the baby starts to take their first steps and develop their walking skills.

When choosing baby booties, it is important to consider factors such as size, material, and ease of use. The booties should fit the baby's feet comfortably without being too tight or too loose. The material should be soft, breathable, and hypoallergenic to prevent any irritation or discomfort. Additionally, booties with easy closures, such as Velcro or elastic bands, make it convenient for parents to put them on and take them off.

Overall, baby booties are an essential accessory for infants and young children. They provide warmth, protection, and support to the baby's feet, ensuring their comfort and safety. With a wide range of styles and designs available, parents can choose booties that not only serve their practical purpose but also add a touch of cuteness and style.

Springtime rompers are a popular fashion choice during the spring season. These one-piece outfits are perfect for those looking for a comfortable and stylish option. They typically feature shorts or cropped pants attached to a top, creating a seamless and effortless look.

One of the main advantages of springtime rompers is their versatility. They can be dressed up or down depending on the occasion. For a casual day out, pair a romper with some sneakers and a denim jacket. This creates a laid-back and trendy look that is perfect for running errands or meeting up with friends. On the other hand, for a more formal event, opt for a romper in a dressier fabric such as silk or satin. Pair it with some heels and statement jewelry to elevate the outfit and make it suitable for a night out or a special occasion.

Another great aspect of springtime rompers is their ability to flatter a variety of body types. With different styles and cuts available, there is a romper out there for everyone. For those with a petite frame, opt for a romper with a higher waistline to create the illusion of longer legs. If you have a curvier figure, look for rompers with a looser fit or ones that cinch at the waist to accentuate your curves. Additionally, rompers with V-necklines can help elongate the neck and create a more balanced silhouette.

When it comes to patterns and colors, springtime rompers offer a wide range of options. Floral prints are a popular choice during this season, as they perfectly capture the essence of spring. Pastel colors such as blush pink, mint green, and baby blue are also commonly seen in springtime rompers, as they evoke a sense of freshness and renewal. However, if you prefer a more minimalist look, there are also solid-colored rompers available in neutral tones such as white, beige, and black.

In terms of fabric, springtime rompers are typically made from lightweight materials such as cotton or linen. This ensures breathability and comfort, making them ideal for warmer weather. Additionally, these fabrics are easy to care for and can be machine washed, making them a practical choice for everyday wear.

Overall, springtime rompers are a versatile and stylish option for the spring season. Whether you're attending a casual gathering or a formal event, there is a romper out there to suit your style and body type. With their comfortable fit and trendy designs, they are a must-have addition.

Summery Sun Hats are a type of hat specifically designed to provide protection from the sun's harmful rays while also keeping you cool and comfortable during hot summer days. These hats are typically made from lightweight and breathable materials such as straw, cotton, or linen, allowing air to circulate and prevent overheating.

One of the key features of summery sun hats is their wide brim, which provides ample shade to shield your face, neck, and shoulders from direct sunlight. The brim also helps to reduce glare and protect your eyes from harmful UV rays. Some sun hats even have an extended brim at the back to offer additional protection to the neck and upper back.

Another important aspect of summery sun hats is their adjustable fit. Many hats come with an adjustable strap or drawstring that allows you to customize the fit according to your head size and comfort level. This ensures that the hat stays securely in place even during outdoor activities or on windy days.

Summery sun hats come in a variety of styles and designs to suit different preferences and occasions. From classic wide-brimmed floppy hats to trendy fedoras and bucket hats, there is a sun hat for every fashion taste. Some hats also feature decorative elements such as ribbons, bows, or colorful patterns, adding a touch of style to your summer outfits.

In addition to their sun protection benefits, summery sun hats are also practical accessories. They are lightweight and easy to pack, making them ideal for travel or beach vacations. Many hats are also crushable or foldable, allowing you to easily store them in your bag without losing their shape.

Overall, summery sun hats are a must-have accessory for anyone who wants to enjoy the outdoors while staying protected from the sun. With their stylish designs, adjustable fit, and sun-blocking features, these hats offer both fashion and function. So, whether you're lounging by the pool, exploring a new city, or attending a summer event, don't forget to grab your summery sun hat to stay cool, comfortable, and sun-safe.

Pacifier clips are small accessories designed to keep pacifiers securely attached to a baby's clothing or bib. They are typically made of a durable material, such as plastic or fabric, and feature a clip on one end and a loop or ring on the other end to hold the pacifier.

These clips are incredibly useful for parents and caregivers as they help prevent pacifiers from getting lost or dropped on the floor. By attaching the clip to the baby's clothing, the pacifier remains within easy reach and can be quickly retrieved when needed. This is especially beneficial when out and about, as it eliminates the need to constantly search for a pacifier or carry multiple spares.

In addition to their practicality, pacifier clips also offer a range of other benefits. They can help soothe and comfort babies by providing easy access to their pacifiers, which can help calm them down and reduce fussiness. This is particularly helpful during nap times or when the baby is feeling irritable.

Furthermore, pacifier clips can also promote good hygiene. By keeping the pacifier attached to the baby's clothing, it reduces the risk of it falling onto dirty surfaces or being exposed to germs. This is especially important for newborns and young infants whose immune systems are still developing.

When choosing a pacifier clip, there are several factors to consider. Firstly, it is important to ensure that the clip is strong and secure, as it will be holding the pacifier in place. The clip should have a firm grip but also be gentle on the baby's clothing to avoid causing any damage.

Additionally, the length of the pacifier clip should be appropriate for the baby's age and size. It should be long enough to allow the baby to comfortably reach the pacifier, but not too long that it poses a safety hazard. Some pacifier clips also come with adjustable lengths, allowing for customization based on the baby's needs.

Lastly, the design and aesthetics of the pacifier clip can also be considered. Many brands offer a wide range of colors, patterns, and themes to choose from, allowing parents to find a clip that matches their baby's style or nursery decor.

Overall, pacifier clips are a practical and convenient accessory for parents and caregivers. They provide a simple solution to keep pacifiers within reach, promote good hygiene, and offer soothing comfort to babies.

Stuffed animals, also known as plush toys or soft toys, are a popular type of toy that are loved by children and adults alike. These toys are typically made from soft materials such as fabric or plush and are filled with stuffing, usually made from polyester fibers or cotton. Stuffed animals come in a wide variety of shapes, sizes, and designs, ranging from traditional teddy bears to animals, characters from movies or cartoons, and even mythical creatures.

One of the main reasons why stuffed animals are so beloved is their cuddly and huggable nature. The softness and squishiness of these toys make them perfect companions for children, providing them with comfort and a sense of security. Many children form strong emotional attachments to their stuffed animals, often treating them as friends or confidants. Stuffed animals can also be used as a tool for teaching children about empathy and nurturing, as they can pretend to care for and take care of their plush companions.

Stuffed animals are not only popular among children, but they also hold a special place in the hearts of adults. Many adults collect stuffed animals as a hobby or for sentimental reasons. These toys can evoke feelings of nostalgia and remind adults of their childhood or special memories. Stuffed animals can also serve as decorative items, adding a touch of whimsy and charm to any room.

In addition to their emotional appeal, stuffed animals also offer a range of developmental benefits for children. Playing with stuffed animals can help improve fine motor skills as children manipulate and grasp the toys. They can also enhance imaginative play, as children create stories and scenarios involving their plush companions. Stuffed animals can also be used as a tool for teaching children about different animals, as they can learn about different species and their characteristics through play.

Furthermore, stuffed animals can provide comfort and support during difficult times. Many children and adults turn to their stuffed animals for solace during times of stress, anxiety, or illness. The soft and comforting nature of these toys can help provide a sense of calm and security, offering a source of emotional support.

In conclusion, stuffed animals are much more than just toys. They hold a special place in the hearts of both children and adults, providing comfort, companionship, and a range of developmental benefits. Whether used for play, decoration, or emotional support, stuffed animals continue to bring joy and happiness to people of all ages.

INTRODUCTION

I don't have a famous love story of how I learned to crochet from a well-known designer or from a loving relative, but my story is personal, and it is what inspires me to design every day. My daughter had received a how-to-crochet-a-scarf kit for Christmas one year and wanted me to teach her how to crochet. I had no idea where to start, but luckily a three-step learner's guide was included, so I taught myself to crochet so that I could teach my daughter. Once I started, I was "hooked"! I loved teaching her to crochet and watching the single strand of yarn turn into something I could use. I soon realized how much I enjoyed crocheting and designing new items.

Through my newfound hobby, I created a top-selling online pattern business, RAKJpatterns, with the goal of offering fresh, creative designs using basic stitches. Since teaching myself and my daughter how to crochet, I have taught countless friends and thousands more via the Internet. I even started an online subscription site, to encourage others to crochet and try new patterns and techniques.

I enjoy designing with fun colors and mixing different stitches to create one-of-a-kind items that are perfect for the sweet new baby in your life or to give as thoughtful, hand-stitched gifts at baby showers for friends and family.

I want this book to be a go-to guide for someone who has never crocheted before, so in addition to the patterns, I've included everything you need to know to crochet them. At the back of the book, you will find photo tutorials for everything from holding a crochet hook to making a chain stitch to double crochet decreases to stitching crocheted pieces together.

You'll find patterns for all different levels of crocheters in this collection. But no matter the level, each pattern is designed to be irresistible! Whether you're a beginner or an experienced crocheter, every pattern you make should be a delight, and the designs in this book are guaranteed to be just that!

I have five children, so I understand that buying cute clothes and hats that your baby will outgrow in just a few months is an indulgence not everyone can afford. But when you can crochet them yourself, and they are this quick and easy to make, the sky is the limit! So pick up your hook, and get ready to crochet!

Some Tips for Reading the Patterns

* When a number is before the command, such as 3hdc, you will work in the SAME stitch.

* When a number is after the command, such as hdc3, you will work that command in that number of following stitches.

* The number in parentheses at the end of a round or row is the TOTAL number of stitches for that round or row.

Chevron Hat and Diaper Cover Set

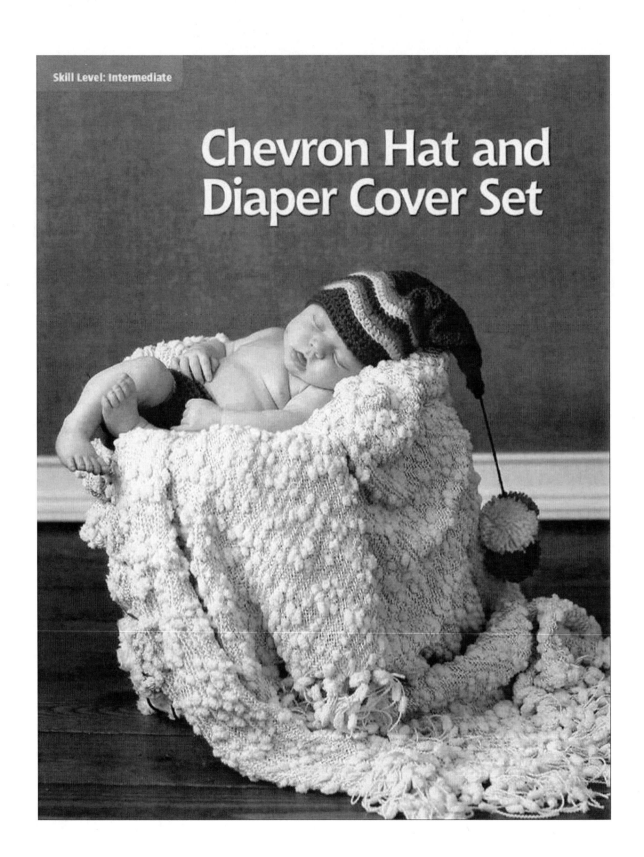

The chevron pattern is simple and easy to create, and this hat and diaper cover will be perfect accessories for your new little one. Make in a variety of colors for boys or girls and be the highlight of any baby shower.

Finished Measurements
Newborn: Hat circumference, 12"; Hat height, 10"
Diaper Cover: Waist, 12.5"
(For other sizes, see Notes.)

Yarn

- Baby Bee Sweet Delight Baby Yarn, light worsted weight #3 yarn, 60% acrylic/40% polyamide (377 yd/4 oz per skein)
    - 1 skein #90 Grape Jelly (Color A)
    - 1 skein #33 Little Princess (Color B)
    - 1 skein #70 Infant Teal (Color C)

Hook and Other Materials

• H-5.0mm hook or size needed to obtain gauge
• Yarn needle

Gauge

18 sts and 10 rows in sc = 4" square

Hat Notes

1. The hat is worked in rows.
2. The ch3 at the beginning of row counts as a stitch.
3. When you change yarns, you will carry the old yarn, not fasten it off. That will allow you to simply pick the yarn up later, with no ends to weave in. For a tutorial, see page 117.
4. See page 112 for a tutorial on Double Crochet Decrease (dc dec) and page 120 for making a pom.
5. The hat size can be naturally altered, using the same pattern, by a) using a larger hook, b) using a heavier weight yarn such as medium worsted weight #4, or c) using both a larger hook and a heavier yarn weight.

Diaper Cover Notes

1. The diaper cover pattern is worked in rows, as a single panel.
2. The ch3 at the beginning of each row counts as a stitch.
3. See page 112 for tutorial on Double Crochet Decrease (dc dec).
4. After the panel is complete, you will sew the 2 sides together to form the base of the diaper cover.
5. The leg opening and waist details will be added after the panel is sewn together.
6. If you tightly slip stitch around the leg holes and waist, the fabric will be tight and difficult to stretch.
7. The size of the diaper cover can be naturally altered, using the same pattern, by a) using a larger hook, b) using a heavier weight yarn such as medium worsted weight #4, or c) using both a larger hook and a heavier yarn weight.

Special Technique

At times you will be instructed to work in the front loop only (flo) or the back loop only (blo) of a stitch. Doing this creates texture in the fabric. See page 107 for a tutorial.

Hat

Using Color A, ch75.

Row 1: Turn, dc in fourth chain from hook, dc in each chain to end (72 sts).

Row 2: Turn, drop Color A (see Notes), join Color B, ch3, dc in same stitch as ch3 in blo (see Special Technique), dc3, dc dec (see Notes) twice, dc3, *2dc in next 2 stitches, dc3, dc dec twice, dc3, repeat from* to second to last stitch, 2dc in last stitch (72 sts).

Row 3: Turn, drop Color B, join Color C, ch3, dc in same stitch as ch3 in flo (see Special Technique), dc3, dc dec twice, dc3, *2dc in next 2 stitches, dc3, dc dec twice, dc3, repeat from* to second to last stitch, 2dc in last stitch (72 sts).

Row 4: Turn, drop Color C, join Color A, ch3, dc in same stitch as ch3 in blo, dc3, dc dec twice, dc3, *2dc in next 2 stitches, dc3, dc dec twice, dc3, repeat from* to second to last stitch, 2dc in last stitch (72 sts).

Row 5: Turn, drop Color A, join Color B, ch3, dc in same stitch as ch3 in flo, dc3, dc dec twice, dc3, *2dc in next 2 stitches, dc3, dc dec twice, dc3, repeat from* to second to last stitch, 2dc in last stitch (72 sts).

Current progress at the end of Row 6.

Row 6: Turn, drop Color B, join Color C, ch3, dc in same stitch as ch3 in blo, dc3, dc dec twice, dc3, *2dc in next 2 stitches, dc3, dc dec twice, dc3, repeat from* to second to last stitch, 2dc in last stitch (72 sts).

Row 7: Turn, drop Color C, join Color A, ch3, dc in same stitch as ch3 in flo, dc3, dc dec twice, dc3, *2dc in next 2 stitches, dc3, dc dec twice, dc3, repeat from* to second to last stitch, 2dc in last stitch (72 sts).

Continue with Color A to the end.

Row 8: Turn, ch3, dc5, dc dec, *dc6, dc dec, repeat from* across (63 sts).

Row 9: Turn, ch3, dc in next stitch and across (63 sts). Bottom row of hat has been completed. Fasten off. Turn panel so that wrong side is facing you with Row 9 at the bottom. Join Color A with a sl st at the top right stitch and continue with Row 10.

Row 10: Ch3, dc5, dc dec, *dc6, dc dec, repeat from* to end (63 sts).

Row 11: Turn, ch3, dc in next stitch and across (63 sts).

Row 12: Turn, ch3, dc4, dc dec, *dc5, dc dec, repeat from* to end (54 sts).

Row 13: Turn, ch3, dc in next stitch and across (54 sts).

Row 14: Turn, ch3, dc3, dc dec, *dc4, dc dec, repeat from* to end (45 sts).

Row 15: Turn, ch3, dc in next stitch and across (45 sts).

Row 16: Turn, ch3, dc2, dc dec, *dc3, dc dec, repeat from* to end (36 sts).
Row 17: Turn, ch3, dc in next stitch and across (36 sts).
Row 18 Turn, ch3, dc, dc dec, *dc2, dc dec, repeat from* to end (27 sts).
Row 19: Turn, ch3, dc in next stitch and across (27 sts).
Row 20: Turn, ch3, dc dec twice, *dc, dc dec, repeat from* to end (18 sts).
Row 21: Turn, ch3, dc in next stitch and across (18 sts).
Row 22: Turn, ch1, dc dec across (9 sts).
Row 23: Turn, ch3, dc in next stitch and across (9 sts).
Row 24: Turn, ch3, dc dec, dc, dc dec, dc, dc dec (6 sts).
Row 25: Turn, ch3, dc in next stitch and across (6 sts).
Fasten off, leaving a long tail to sew together.

Using the yarn needle, sew the hat together from the bottom to the top with a basic stitch (see page 120).

Tail and Poms

For the tail, cut three 12" long strands of Color A.

Knot strands together at one end, and attach to the inside top of hat. Braid the strands, leaving 1" unbraided. Knot the braid to secure.

Make 1 pom in each color (see Notes). Attach a pom to each strand at the end of the braid. Hat is complete.

Current progress on hat after Row 25.

Diaper Cover

Using Color A, ch31.

Row 1: Dc in fourth chain from hook and across (28 sts).

Rows 2–10: Turn, ch3, dc in next stitch and across (28 sts).

Row 11: Turn, do not ch, dc dec, dc24, dc dec (see Notes; 26 sts).

Row 12: Turn, dc dec, dc22, dc dec (24 sts).

Row 13: Turn, dc dec 2 times, dc16, dc dec 2 times (20 sts).

Row 14: Turn, dc dec 2 times, dc12, dc dec 2 times (16 sts).

Rows 15–23: Turn, ch3, dc in next stitch and across (16 sts).

Row 24: Turn, ch3, dc in same stitch as ch3, 2dc in next stitch, dc12, 2dc in last 2 stitches (20 sts).

Row 25: Turn, ch3, dc in same stitch as ch3, 2dc in next stitch, dc16, 2dc in last 2 stitches (24 sts).

Row 26: Turn, ch3, dc in same stitch as ch3, dc24, 2dc in last stitch (26 sts).

Row 27: Turn, ch3, dc in same stitch as ch3, dc 26, 2dc in last stitch (28 sts).

Rows 28–36: Turn, ch3, dc in next stitch and across (28 sts).

Fasten off.

Fold the panel in half, aligning Rows 1 and 36.

With the yarn needle, starting at the top, sew each side down to Row 12, leaving an opening for the leg holes.

Fasten off.

Current progress on diaper cover after Row 36.

Leg Hole Detail

Turn diaper cover right side out, join Color C at the top seam of the leg hole. Ch1, and working to the left on each side, use the ends of the rows as stitches and sc around, sl st to ch1 to join (30 sts).

Fasten off Color C, join Color B, ch1, loosely sl st in each stitch around, sl st to ch1 to join.

Fasten off.

Waist Detail

At waist opening, join Color C, ch1, sc in each stitch around, sl st to ch1 to join.

Fasten off Color C, join Color B, ch1, loosely sl st in each stitch around, sl st to ch1 to join.

Fasten off. Weave in all ends.

Wrap your baby in this textured pod, and he will stay warm and cozy.

Finished Measurements
Length: 15"; Circumference: 35"

Yarn

- Yarn Bee Riot Eyelash, super bulky weight #6 yarn, 58% polyamide/42% polyester (109 yd/3.5 oz per skein) 1 skein #3 Sea Leaves **Hook and Other Materials**
- N-9.0mm hook or size needed to obtain gauge

Gauge
7 sts and 5 rows in dc = 4" square

Notes

1. The pod is worked from the bottom up in the round.
2. When joining end of each round, sl st to third chain of the ch3.
3. See page 112 for a tutorial on Double Crochet Decrease (dc dec).
4. If a tighter fit is desired, weave the yarn through Round 10 like a drawstring and tie it gently.

Baby Pod

Ch4, sl st to first chain to create a ring.

Round 1: Ch3, 12dc in ring, sl st to ch3 (see Notes) to join (12 sts).

Round 2: Ch3, 2dc in each stitch to complete round, sl st to ch3 to join (24 sts).

Round 3: Ch3, 2dc in next stitch, *dc, 2dc in next stitch, repeat from* to complete round, sl st to ch3 to join (36 sts).

Round 4: Ch3, dc, 2dc in next stitch, *dc2, 2dc in next stitch, repeat from* to complete round, sl st to ch3 to join (48 sts).

Round 5: Ch3, dc2, 2dc in next stitch, *dc3, 2dc in next stitch, repeat from* to complete round, sl st to ch3 to join (60 sts).

Rounds 6–8: Ch3, dc in each stitch to complete round, sl st to first ch3 to join (60 sts).

Round 9: Ch3, dc2, dc dec (see Notes), *dc3, dc dec, repeat from* to complete round, sl st to ch3 to join (48 sts).

Round 10: Ch3, dc, dc dec, *dc2, dc dec, repeat from* to complete round, sl st to ch3 to join (36 sts).

Rounds 11–12: Ch1, sc in each stitch to complete round (36 sts).

Fasten off. Weave in ends.

This dainty top will be ever so sweet on your baby girl! It's perfect for the warmer months when worn plain, or you can dress it up with a shrug or cardigan in the cooler months.

Finished Measurements

3–6 months: Chest, 8.5"; Length, 7.5"

6–9 months: Chest, 11"; Length, 10"

Yarn

- Baby Bee Sweet Delight Baby Yarn, light worsted weight #3 yarn, 60% acrylic/40% polyamide (377 yd/4 oz per skein)

  1 skein #70 Infant Teal (Color A)

  1 skein #33 Little Princess (Color B)

  1 skein #90 Grape Jelly (Color C)

Hook and Other Materials

• E-3.50mm hoo or size needed to obtain gauge
• Yarn needle

Gauge

16 sts and 8 rows in dc = 3" square

Notes

1. The garment is worked from the top down in rows.
2. The ch2 at the beginning of each row is not a counted stitch.
3. The sl st at the end of each round to the first dc stitch creates a seamless join.
4. See page 113 for a tutorial on Front Post Double Crochet (fpdc).

Special Technique

Front Post Treble (fptr) (See page 115 for a photo tutorial for treble crochet and page 113 for crocheting on the front post.) 1. Yarn over 3 times, push hook through front post of stitch, yarn over, and pull through: 4 loops on hook.

2. Yarn over, pull through first 2 loops on hook: 3 loops on hook.

3. Yarn over, pull through 2 loops on hook: 2 loops on hook.

4. Yarn over, pull through last 2 loops on hook. Front post treble is complete.

Top

3–6 Months

Using Color A, ch93.

Round 1: Dc in fourth chain from hook and across, sl st to first dc stitch (not loose chains) to join (88 sts).

Round 2: Turn ch2, dc in same stitch used to join the row, dc in each stitch across, sl st to first dc stitch to join (88 sts).

Rounds 3–9: Repeat Round 2.

Round 10: Turn, ch3, dc in same stitch used to join round, dc, *skip 2 stitches, (2dc, ch1, 2dc) in next stitch, skip 2 stitches, dc3, and repeat from* to complete round, sl st to ch3 to join (88 sts).

Round 11: Turn, ch3, skip first stitch, fpdc (see Notes) in next 2 stitches, (2dc, ch1, 2dc) in ch1 space, *skip next 2 dc, fpdc in next 3 stitches, (2dc, ch1, 2dc) in next ch1 space, repeat from* and end on fpdc3. Sl st to ch3 to join (88 stitches).

Round 12: Repeat Round 11.

Rounds 13–15: Turn, ch3, skip first stitch, fpdc in next 2 stitches, (3dc, ch1, 3dc) in ch1 space, *skip next 2 dc, fpdc in next 3 stitches, (3dc, ch1, 3dc) in next ch1 space, repeat from* and end on fpdc3. Sl st to ch3 to join (98 sts).

Rounds 16–18: Turn, ch3, skip first stitch, fpdc in next 2 stitches, (4dc, ch1, 4dc) in ch1 space, *skip next 2 dc, fpdc in next 3 stitches, (4dc, ch1, 4dc) in next ch1 space, repeat from* and end on fpdc3. Sl st to ch3 to join (108 sts).

Rounds 19–21: Turn, ch3, skip first stitch, fptr (see <u>Special Technique</u>) in next 2 stitches, (5dc, ch1, 5dc) in ch1 space, *skip next 2 dc, fptr in next 3 stitches, (5dc, ch1, 5dc) in next ch1 space, repeat from* and end on fptr3. Sl st to ch3 to join (118 sts).

Fasten off. Weave in ends.

6–9 Months

Using Color A, ch109.

Round 1: Dc in fourth chain from hook and across, sl st to first dc stitch (not loose chains) to join (104 sts).

Round 2: Turn ch2, dc in same stitch used to join row, dc in each stitch across, sl st to first dc stitch to join (104 sts).

Rounds 3–14: Repeat Round 2.

Round 15: Turn, ch3, dc in same stitch used to join row, dc, *skip 2 stitches, (2dc, ch1, 2dc) in next stitch, skip 2 stitches, dc3, repeat from* to complete round, sl st to ch3 to join (104 sts).

Round 16: Turn, ch3, skip first stitch, fpdc (see <u>Notes</u>) in next 2 stitches, (2dc, ch1, 2dc) in ch1 space, *skip next 2 dc, fpdc in next 3 stitches, (2dc, ch1, 2dc) in next ch1 space, repeat from* and end on fpdc3. Sl st to ch3 to join (104 stitches).

Rounds 17–18: Repeat Round 16.

Rounds 19–21: Turn, ch3, skip first stitch, fpdc in next 2 stitches, (3dc, ch1, 3dc) in ch1 space, *skip next 2 dc, fpdc in next 3 stitches, (3dc, ch1, 3dc) in next ch1 space, repeat from* and end on fpdc3. Sl st to first ch3 to join (114 sts).

Rounds 22–25: Turn, ch3, skip first stitch, fpdc in next 2 stitches, (4dc, ch1, 4dc) in ch1 space, *skip next 2 dc, fpdc in next 3 stitches, (4dc, ch1, 4dc) in next ch1 space, repeat from* and end on fpdc3. Sl st to ch3 to join (124 sts).

Rounds 26–29: Turn, ch3, skip first stitch, fptr (see Special Technique on page 9) in next 2 stitches, (5dc, ch1, 5dc) in ch1 space, *skip next 2 dc, fptr in next 3 stitches, (5dc, ch1, 5dc) in next ch1 space, repeat from* and end on fptr3. Sl st to ch3 to join (134 sts).

Fasten off. Weave in ends.

Flowers

Large Middle Flower (make 1)

Using Color B, ch45.

Turn, dc in fourth chain from hook, ch1, dc in same stitch, *ch1, (dc, ch1, dc) in next stitch, repeat from* to complete row.

Fasten off, leaving a long tail to sew into place. Roll into a round flower and secure tightly with yarn needle. Sew onto center of the top.

Small Side Flowers (make 2)

Using Color C, ch25.

Turn, sc in first chain from hook and across.

Fasten off, leaving a long tail to sew into place. Roll into a small round flower and secure tightly with yarn needle. Sew one to each side of large flower.

Straps (make 2)

Measure 2" in from each side of top and mark stitch. In each marked stitch, join Color A with a slip stitch and ch50. Fasten off. Weave in ends. Tie loosely.

Mix and match colors to create the perfect zigzag beanie. This design will be great for girls with the adorable flower and awesome for boys with a primary color mix!

Finished Measurements

Newborn: Circumference, 12–14"; Hat height, 5"

63–6 months: Circumference, 14–17"; Hat height, 5.5"

9–12 months: Circumference, 16–19"; Hat height, 6"

Yarn

• I Love This Cotton!, medium worsted weight #4 yarn, 100% cotton (180 yd/3.5 oz per skein)

        1 skein #254 Rosy (Color A)

        1 skein #12 Buttercup (Color B)

Hook and Other Materials

• F-3.75mm hook or size needed to obtain gauge
• Stitch marker (optional)

Gauge
14 sts and 16 rows in sc = 3" square

Notes

1. The hat is worked from the top down continuously in the round. If you like, mark the first stitch of the round with a stitch marker for reference.
2. When you change yarns, you will carry the old yarn, not fasten it off. That will allow you to simply pick the yarn up later with no ends to weave in. For a tutorial, see page 117.
3. See page 110 for a tutorial on Half Double Crochet (hdc).
4. The flowers are optional.

Hat

Newborn

Using Color A, ch2.
Round 1: 8sc in first chain (8 sts).
Round 2: Working continuously in the round, 2sc in each stitch (16 sts).
Round 3: *Sc, 2sc in next stitch, repeat from* to complete round (24 sts).
Round 4: *Sc2, 2sc in next stitch, repeat from* to complete round (32 sts).
Round 5: *Sc3, 2sc in next stitch, repeat from* to complete round (40 sts).

Rounds 6–7: Sc in each stitch (48 sts).

Round 8: Sc7, drop Color A, pick up Color B (see Notes), sc1, *drop Color B, pick up Color A, sc7, drop Color A, pick up Color B, sc1, repeat from* to complete round (48 sts).

Round 9: *Drop Color B, pick up Color A, sc5, drop Color A, pick up Color B, sc3, repeat from* to complete round (48 sts).

Round 10: *Drop Color B, pick up Color A, sc3, drop Color A, pick up Color B, sc5, repeat from* to complete round (48 sts).

Round 11: *Drop Color B, pick up Color A, sc1, drop Color A, pick up Color B, sc7, repeat from* to complete round (48 sts).

Rounds 12–20: Using Color B, sc in each stitch (48 sts).

Fasten off Color B, pick up Color A.

Rounds 21–24: Sc in each stitch (48 sts). To finish, sl st to first stitch of round.

Fasten off. Weave in ends.

3–6 Months

Using Color A, ch2.

Round 1: 8sc in first chain (8 sts).

Round 2: Working continuously in the round, 2sc in each stitch (16 sts).

Round 3: *Sc, 2sc in next stitch, repeat from* to complete round (24 sts).

Round 4: *Sc2, 2sc in next stitch, repeat from* to complete round (32 sts).

Round 5: *Sc3, 2sc in next stitch, repeat from* to complete round (40 sts).

Round 6: *Sc4, 2sc in next stitch, repeat from* to complete round (48 sts).

Round 7: *Sc5, 2sc in next stitch, repeat from* to complete round (56 sts).

Rounds 8–9: Sc in each stitch (56 sts).

Round 10: Sc7, drop Color A, pick up Color B (see Notes), sc1, *drop Color B, pick up Color A, sc7, drop Color A, pick up Color B, sc1, repeat from* to complete round (56 sts).

Round 11: *Drop Color B, pick up Color A, sc5, drop Color A, pick up Color B, sc3, repeat from* to complete round (56 sts).

Round 12: *Drop Color B, pick up Color A, sc 3, drop Color A, pick up Color B, sc5, repeat from* to complete round (56 sts).

Round 13: *Drop Color B, pick up Color A, sc1, drop Color A, pick up Color B, sc7, repeat from* to complete round (56 sts).

Rounds 14–24: Using Color B, sc in each stitch (56 sts).

Fasten off Color B, pick up Color A.

Rounds 25–28: Sc in each stitch (56 sts). To finish, sl st to first stitch of round.

Fasten off. Weave in ends.

9–12 Months

Using Color A, ch2.

Round 1: 8sc in first chain (8 sts).

Round 2: Working continuously in the round, 2sc in each stitch (16 sts).

Round 3: *Sc, 2sc in next stitch, repeat from* to complete round (24 sts).

Round 4: *Sc2, 2sc in next stitch, repeat from* to complete round (32 sts).

Round 5: *Sc3, 2sc in next stitch, repeat from* to complete round (40 sts).

Round 6: *Sc4, 2sc in next stitch, repeat from* to complete round (48 sts).

Round 7: *Sc5, 2sc in next stitch, repeat from* to complete round (56 sts).

Round 8: *Sc6, 2sc in next stitch, repeat from* to complete round (64 sts).

Round 9: *Sc7, 2sc in next stitch, repeat from* to complete round (72 sts).

Rounds 10–11: Sc in each stitch (72 sts).

Round 12: Sc7, drop Color A, pick up Color B (see Notes), sc1, *drop Color B, pick up Color A, sc7, drop Color A, pick up Color B, sc1, repeat from* to complete round (72 sts).

Round 13: *Drop Color B, pick up Color A, sc5, drop Color A, pick up Color B, sc3, repeat from* to complete round (72 sts).

Round 14: *Drop Color B, pick up Color A, sc 3, drop Color A, pick up Color B, sc5, repeat from* to complete round (72 sts).

Round 15: *Drop Color B, pick up Color A, sc1, drop Color A, pick up Color B, sc7, repeat from* to complete round (72 sts).

Rounds 16–28: Using Color B, sc in each stitch (72 sts). Fasten off Color B, pick up Color A.

Rounds 29–32: Sc in each stitch (72 sts). To finish, sl st to first stitch of round.

Fasten off. Weave in ends.

Flowers (optional)

Back Flower

Using Color A, ch3.

Round 1: 8hdc (see Notes) in first chain (8 sts).

Round 2: Working continuously in the round, 2hdc in each stitch (16 sts).

Round 3: *Hdc, 2hdc in next stitch, repeat from* to complete round (24 sts).

Round 4: Ch4, sl st to same stitch, ch4 in next stitch, sl st to same stitch, repeat from * to complete round, sl st to first stitch to join.

Fasten off. Weave in ends.

Middle Flower

Using Color A, ch3.

Round 1: 8hdc in first chain (8 sts).

Round 2: Working continuously in the round, 2hdc in each stitch (16 sts).

Round 3: Ch4, sl st to same stitch, *ch4 in next stitch, sl st to same stitch, repeat from * to complete the round, sl st to first stitch of round to join.

Fasten off and weave in ends.

Top Flower
Using Color A, ch3.
Round 1: 8hdc in first chain (8 sts).
Round 2: Ch4, sl st to same stitch, *ch4 in next stitch, sl st to same stitch, repeat from * to complete round, sl st to first stitch of round to join.
Fasten off. Weave in ends.

Finishing

Using yarn needle, sew centers of the flowers together and secure to hat. Weave in ends.

Your baby will never have cold feet with these cozy socks on. They are soft, durable, and absolutely the best thing to snuggle your li'l one's feet. They can be made in multiple sizes. Crochet several pairs now so they can be worn all year round as your baby grows.

Finished Measurements

Toe to back of heel
Newborn: 3"
3–6 months: 3.5"
9–12 months: 4"

Yarn

- Deborah Norville Serenity Sock Yarn, super fine #1 yarn (50% super wash merino wool/25% rayon/25% nylon (230 yd/1.7 oz per skein)
    - 1 skein #DN125-01 Harlequin

Hook and Other Materials

- C-2.75mm hook or size needed to obtain gauge
- Yarn needle
- Stitch marker (optional)

Gauge

13 sts and 16 rows in sc = 2" square

Notes

1. The socks are worked from the toe up continuously in the round, except for the heel. If you like, use a stitch marker to mark the first stitch of the round for reference.

2. The foot length can be altered by increasing or decreasing the number of rounds before beginning the heel.

3. The cuff can be extended by adding rounds until the desired length is reached.

4. When sewing the heel and toe sections, use the same color as the surrounding area so that the join appears seamless.

5. When sewing the toe, make sure it is lined up correctly with the heel in the back center and not on the side, or the seam will be sideways and not flat when worn.

6. See page 109 for a tutorial on Single Crochet Decrease (sc dec).
7. See page 113 for a tutorial on Front Post Double Crochet (fpdc) and page 114 for Back Post Double Crochet (bpdc). When completed as instructed for the cuff, these stitches create the ribbing.

The ribbing allows the cuff to hug the ankle instead of fitting loosely.

Socks (make 2)

Newborn

Toe/Foot

Ch10, sl st to first chain to create a ring.

Round 1: Working continuously in the round, dc in each chain (10 sts).
Round 2: 2sc in each stitch (20 sts).
Rounds 3–16: Sc in each stitch (20 sts).

Heel

Row 17: Turn, ch1, sc10 (10 sts).
Rows 18–22: Turn, ch1, turn, sc to end of row (10 sts). A "flap" has been created.

Ankle

Row 23: Ch1, working on side of flap, use ends of rows as stitches and sc6, then sc10 across top of the flap, then sc6 down other side of flap using ends of rows as stitches (22 sts).

Round 24: Do not work over the 10 stitches on end of flap. Skip the ch1 and locate first sc from beginning of Row 23; this is where Round 24 will begin. Sc dec (see <u>Notes</u>) using first 2 stitches, sc20 to complete round (21 sts).

Round 25: Sc dec using first 2 stitches, sc19 to complete round (20 sts).

Rounds 26–27: Working continuously in the round, sc in each stitch (20 sts).

Cuff

Round 28: Ch3, *fpdc2, bpdc, repeat from* to last stitch, bpdc using first ch3 to complete round (20 sts).

Rounds 29–30: *Fpdc2, bpdc, repeat from* to complete each round. The stitches will line up and create a ribbing effect.

Round 31: *Fpdc2, bpdc, repeat from* to complete round, sl st to next stitch to finish (20 sts).

With the yarn needle, sew the toe and heel openings closed.

The seam is worked in purple here so you can see how to complete the stitching from the inside, but use the same color as the surrounding area so that the seam is not seen when you are finished.

3–6 Months

Toe/Foot

Ch10, sl st to first chain to create a ring.

Round 1: Working continuously in the round, dc in each chain (10 sts).

Round 2: 2sc in each stitch (20 sts).
Round 3: *Sc, 2sc, repeat from* to complete round (30 sts).
Rounds 4–20: Sc in each stitch (30 sts).

Heel
Row 21: Turn, ch1, sc15 (15 sts).
Rows 22–28: Turn, ch1, sc to end of row (15 sts).
A "flap" has been created.

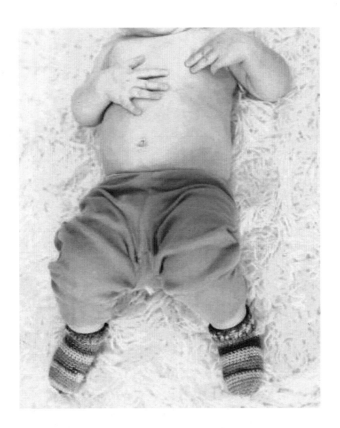

Ankle
Round 29: Ch1, working on side of flap, use ends of rows as stitches and sc8, sc15 across top of flap, and sc8 down other side of flap, using ends of rows as stitches (31 sts).

75

Round 30: Do not work over the 15 stitches on the end of the flap. Skip the ch1 and locate first sc from the beginning of Round 2; this is where Round 30 will begin. Sc dec (see Notes) using first 2 stitches, sc29 to complete round (30 sts).

Rounds 31–32: Working continuously in the round, sc in each stitch (30 sts).

Cuff

Round 33: Ch3, *fpdc2 (see Notes), bpdc (see Notes), repeat from * to last stitch, bpdc using first ch3 to complete round (30 sts).

Rounds 34–35: *Fpdc2, bpdc, repeat from* to complete each round. The stitches will line up and create a ribbing effect.

Round 36: *Fpdc2, bpdc, repeat from* to complete round, sl st to next stitch to finish (30 sts).

Using the yarn needle, sew the toe and heel openings closed.

9–12 Months

Toe/Foot

Ch10, sl st to first chain to create a ring.

Round 1: Working continuously in the round, dc in each chain (10 sts).

Round 2: 2sc in each stitch (20 sts).

Round 3: *Sc, 2sc, repeat from* to complete round (30 sts).

Round 4: *Sc2, 2sc, repeat from* to complete round (40 sts).

Rounds 5–26: Sc in each stitch (40 sts).

Heel

Row 27: Turn, ch1, sc20 (20 sts).

Rows 28–36: Turn, ch1, sc in each stitch to end of row (20 sts).

A "flap" has been created.

Ankle

Round 37: Ch1, working on side of flap, use ends of rows as stitches and sc11, sc20 across top of flap, sc11 down other side of flap, using ends of rows as stitches (42 sts).

Round 38: Do not work over the 20 stitches on the end of flap. Skip the ch1 and locate the first sc from the beginning of Round 37; this is where Round 38 will begin. Sc dec (see Notes) using first 2 stitches, sc39 to complete round

(41 sts).

Round 39: Sc dec using first 2 stitches, sc39 to complete round (40 sts).

Rounds 40–41: Working continuously in the round, sc in each stitch (40 sts).

Cuff

Round 42: Ch3, *fpdc2 (see <u>Notes</u>), bpdc (see <u>Notes</u>), repeat from * to last stitch, bpdc using first ch3 to complete round (40 sts).

Rounds 43–45: *Fpdc2, bpdc, repeat from* to complete each round. The stitches will line up and create a ribbing effect.

Round 46: *Fpdc2, bpdc, repeat from* to complete round, sl st to next stitch to finish (40 sts).

Using the yarn needle, sew the toe and heel openings closed.

Ruffles! Ruffles! Ruffles! By using the Sashay yarn, you can easily create ruffles and add a bit of pizzazz to any accessory. Why be boring when you can be cute?

Finished Measurements

Skirt, Waist

Newborn: 12"

3–6 months: 6"

6–9 months: 18"

9–12 months: 20"

Leg Warmers, Length (without ruffles)

Newborn: 7.5"

3–6 months: 8.5"

6–9 months: 9.5"

9–12 months: 10.5"

Yarn

- Lion Brand Vanna's Choice, medium worsted weight #4 yarn, 100% acrylic (170 yd/3.5 oz per skein)
    1 skein #860-110 Navy (Color A)
- Red Heart Boutique Sashay Yarn, super bulky #6 yarn, 97% acrylic/3% metallic polyester (30 yd/3.5 oz per skein)
    1 skein #1932 Rumba (Color B)

Hook and Other Materials

• H-5.0mm hook or size needed to obtain gauge

Gauge
11 sts and 12 rows in sc = 3" square

Skirt Notes

1. The skirt is worked from the bottom up with Color A. The ruffles (in Color B) are added last.

2. The last round on each size will create the loops for the "belt" to weave through.

Leg Warmer Notes

1. See page 110 for a tutorial on Half Double Crochet (hdc).
2. The length of the leg warmers can be adjusted by increasing or decreasing the number of rounds worked.

Special Techniques

Using Sashay Yarn to Create Ruffles

Stretch the yarn out. The top is a straight line with posts, and the bottom has several "stitches" and is already detailed.

The top row has 2 posts worked approximately every inch. You will use the 2 posts as your "stitch" to create the ruffles. Yarn over the 2 stitches, and sl st through the stitch on the hook. Skip the next "stitch" and yarn over the next. Sl st. Continue to create the ruffle as directed in the pattern.

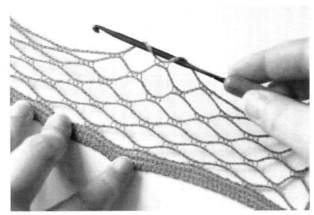

Use the top posts on the Sashay yarn to create the slip stitch.

Front Post Treble (fptr)

(See page 115 for a photo tutorial for treble crochet and page 113 for crocheting on the front post.) 1. Yarn over 3 times, push hook through front post of stitch, yarn over, and pull through: 4 loops on hook.

2. Yarn over, pull through first 2 loops on hook: 3 loops on hook.

3. Yarn over, pull through 2 loops on hook: 2 loops on hook.

4. Yarn over, pull through last 2 loops on hook. Front post treble is complete.

Skirt

Newborn

Using Color A, ch61.

Round 1: Turn, sc in first chain and across, sl st to first stitch to join (60 sts).

Round 2: Ch1, sc in each stitch, do not join (60 sts).

Rounds 3–11: Working continuously in the round, sc in each stitch (60 sts).

Round 12: *Fptr (see Special Techniques on page 19) using post from 3 rows below, sc5, repeat from * to complete round, sl st to first stitch of round to

join.
Fasten off. Weave in ends.

3–6 Months
Using Color A, ch71.
Round 1: Turn, sc in first chain and across, sl st to first stitch to join (70 sts).
Round 2: Ch1, sc in each stitch, do not join (70 sts).
Rounds 3–14: Working continuously in the round, sc in each stitch (70 sts).
Round 15: *Fptr (see Special Techniques on <ins>page 19</ins>) using post from 3 rows below, sc5, repeat from * to complete round, sl st to first stitch of round to join.
Fasten off. Weave in ends.

6–9 Months
Using Color A, ch81.
Round 1: Turn, sc in first chain and across, sl st to first stitch to join (80 sts).
Round 2: Ch1, sc in each stitch, do not join (80 sts).
Rounds 3–19: Working continuously in the round, sc in each stitch (80 sts).
Round 20: *Fptr (see Special Techniques on <ins>page 19</ins>) using post from 3 rows below, sc5, repeat from * to complete round, sl st to first stitch of round to join.
Fasten off. Weave in ends.

9–12 Months
Using Color A, ch91.
Round 1: Turn, sc in first chain and across, sl st to first stitch to join (90 sts).
Round 2: Ch1, sc in each stitch, do not join (90 sts).
Rounds 3–24: Working continuously in the round, sc in each stitch (90 sts).
Round 25: *Fptr (see Special Techniques on <ins>page 19</ins>) using post from 3 rows below, sc5, repeat from * to complete round, sl st to first stitch of round to join.
Fasten off. Weave in ends.

Skirt Ruffles

Join Color B. Following the directions under Special Technique for creating ruffles, sl st 5 rounds. Fasten off. To weave in ends seamlessly, pull the end of the cut yarn to the back and tie securely.

Belt

Starting in the back, weave Color B through the belt loops. Leave a long enough tail to tie into a bow. Cut and tie.

Leg Warmers

Newborn

Using Color A, ch17.

Round 1: Turn, sc in first chain and across, do not join (16 sts).

Rounds 2–18: Working continuously in the round, hdc (see Notes) in each stitch. To finish, sl st to first stitch of round (16 sts).

3–6 Months

Using Color A, ch21.

Round 1: Turn, sc in first chain and across, do not join (20 sts).

Rounds 2–22: Working continuously in the round, hdc (see Notes) in each stitch. To finish, sl st to first stitch of round (20 sts).

6–9 Months

Using Color A, ch25.

Round 1: Turn, sc in first chain and across, do not join (24 sts).

Rounds 2–26: Working continuously in the round, hdc (see Notes) in each stitch. To finish, sl st to first stitch of round (24 sts).

9–12 Months

Using Color A, ch29.

Round 1: Turn, sc in first chain and across, do not join (28 sts).

Rounds 2–30: Working continuously in the round, hdc (see Notes) in each stitch. To finish, sl st to first stitch of round (28 sts).

Leg Warmer Ruffles

Join Color B. Following the directions under Special Techniques on page 19 for creating ruffles, sl st 2 rounds. Fasten off. To weave in ends seamlessly, pull the end of the cut yarn to the back and tie securely.

We all love to see our little ones soar, and now they can do it wearing this sweet aviator cap!

Finished Measurements

Newborn: Circumference, 12–14";
     Hat height, 5.5–6"

3–6 months: Circumference, 14–17";
     Hat height, 6.5–7"

9–12 months: Circumference, 16–19";
     at height, 7.5"

Yarn

- Lion Brand Jiffy, bulky weight #5 yarn, 100% acrylic (135 yd/3 oz per skein)
  - 1 skein #450-126 Espresso (Color A)
  - 1 skein #450-098 Oat (Color B)

Hook and Other Materials • H-5.0mm or size need to obtain gauge

- Yarn needle
- Stitch markers

Gauge

9 sts and 12 rows in sc = 3" square

Notes

1. The hat is worked from the top down continuously in the round. If you like, use a stitch marker to mark the first stitch of the round for reference.
2. See page 109 for the tutorial on Single Crochet Decrease (sc dec).
3. The goggles are made separately and sewn onto hat with a yarn needle.
4. The headband is attached to the goggles, not the hat, so it will stretch when worn.

Hat

Newborn

Using Color A, ch4, sl st to first chain to create a ring.

Round 1: Ch1 (this counts as your first sc), 7sc in ring (8 sts).

Round 2: Working continuously in the round, 2sc in each stitch (16 sts).
Round 3: *Sc, 2sc in next stitch, repeat from* to complete round (24 sts).
Round 4: *Sc2, 2sc in next stitch, repeat from* to complete round (32 sts).
Rounds 5–16: Sc in each stitch (32 sts).
Fasten off and weave in ends.

3–6 Months

Using Color A, ch4, sl st to first chain to create a ring.
Round 1: Ch1 (this counts as your first sc), 7sc in ring (8 sts).
Round 2: Working continuously in the round, 2sc in each stitch (16 sts).
Round 3: *Sc, 2sc in next stitch, repeat from* to complete round (24 sts).
Round 4: *Sc2, 2sc in next stitch, repeat from* to complete round (32 sts).
Round 5: *Sc3, 2sc in next stitch, repeat from* to complete round (40 sts).
Rounds 6–20: Sc in each stitch (40 sts).
Fasten off and weave in ends.

9–12 Months

Using Color A, ch4, sl st to first chain to create a ring.
Round 1: Ch1 (this counts as your first sc), 7sc in ring (8 sts).
Round 2: Working continuously in the round, 2sc in each stitch (16 sts).
Round 3: *Sc, 2sc in next stitch, repeat from* to complete round (24 sts).
Round 4: *Sc2, 2sc in next stitch, repeat from* to complete round (32 sts).
Round 5: *Sc3, 2sc in next stitch, repeat from* to complete round (40 sts).
Round 6: *Sc4, 2sc in next stitch, repeat from* to complete round (48 sts).
Rounds 7–24: Sc in each stitch (48 sts).
Fasten off and weave in ends.

Ear Flaps (make 2)

Fold hat in half and mark opposite sides on the last round with a stitch marker.
Join Color A at marker and follow pattern per size to complete ear flaps.

Newborn

Using Color A, ch1.

Row 1: 6sc (6 sts).

Rows 2–5: Turn, ch1, sc to end of row (6 sts).

Row 6: Turn, sc dec (see Notes), sc2, sc dec (4 sts).

Row 7: Turn, sc dec, sc dec (2 sts).

Fasten off. Weave in ends.

Repeat for flap on opposite side.

3–6 and 9–12 Months

Using Color A, ch1.

Row 1: 8sc (8 sts).

Rows 2–6: Turn, ch1, sc to end of row (8 sts).

Row 7: Turn, sc dec (see Notes), sc4, sc dec (6 sts).

Row 8: Turn, sc dec, sc2, sc dec (4 sts).

Fasten off. Weave in ends.

Repeat for flap on opposite side.

Goggles (all sizes; make 2)

Using Color B, ch20, sl st to first chain to make a ring **Round 1:** Ch1, sc in each chain, sl st to ch1 to join.

Fasten off. Weave in ends.

With yarn needle, sew rings onto the hat in 2 oval shapes, touching at one end to create the goggles. For the nose piece, use Color B and wrap around where the ovals touch 10 times. This will also make the goggles look seamless.

Fasten off. Weave in ends.

Headband

Lay the hat in front of you. Join Color B on outside middle of the right goggle, ch35 (ch40 for 3–6 months/ch45 for 9–12 months), sl st to the middle of the left goggle. Turn the hat and sl st to the stitch below on the goggles. Now, sc in each chain back across the headband. Sl st to the stitch below the first chain made on the right side of goggle. Fasten off. Weave in ends.

Everyone loves a blast from the past, and this Old-School Jacob Vest will do the trick. Make it in any color, for boy or girl, and dress it up with the tie just for fun or a special occasion.

Finished Measurements

6–12 months: Length, 9"; Chest, 11.5"

(For other sizes, see Notes.) **Yarn**

- Lily Sugar 'n Cream, medium worsted weight #4 yarn, 100% cotton (120 yd/2.5 oz per skein)

        2 skeins #00026 Light Blue (Color A)

        1 skein #0004 Ecru (Color B)

        1skein #01130 Warm Brown (Color C)

Hook and Other Materials

- H-5.0mm hook or size needed to obtain gauge
- Yarn needle
- Sewing thread and needle
- 4 medium buttons in coordinating color

Gauge
11 sts and 13 rows in sc = 3" square

Notes

1. The vest is worked in rows as a panel from the left front side to the left back side, and then is seamed on the side to finish.

2. The shoulders are buttoned, not sewn.

3. See page 109 for a tutorial on Single Crochet Decrease (sc dec) and page 107 for working the back loop only (blo) of a stitch.

4. Slip stitch loosely when working the trim.

5. The tie is made separately and then sewn onto the vest.

6. To make this larger, use a 6.5mm crochet hook; to make it smaller, use a 3.5mm hook.

Special Technique
Slip Stitch Decrease (sl st dec)

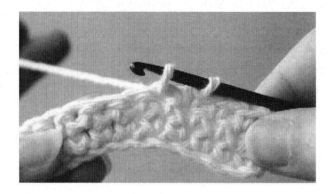

1. Push hook through stitch, yarn over, and pull yarn back through: 2 loops on hook.

2. Push hook through next stitch, yarn over, and pull yarn back through: 3 loops on hook.

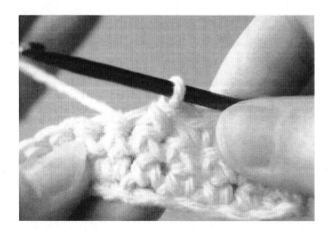

3. Yarn over, pull yarn through all 3 loops. Slip stitch decrease is complete.

Vest

Using Color A, ch19.

Row 1: Turn, sc in first chain and across (18 sts).

Row 2: Turn, ch1, 2sc in first stitch, sc in each stitch across (19 sts).

Row 3: Turn, ch1, sc18, 2sc in last stitch (20 sts).

Row 4: Turn, ch1, 2sc in first stitch, sc in each stitch across (21 sts).

Row 5: Turn, ch1, sc20, 2sc in last stitch (22 sts).

Row 6: Turn, ch1, 2sc in first stitch, sc in each stitch across (23 sts).

Row 7: Turn, ch1, sc22, 2sc in last stitch (24 sts).

Row 8: Turn, ch9, sc in first chain from hook and across (32 sts).

Row 9: Turn, ch1, sc in each stitch across (32 sts).

Rows 10–13: Repeat Row 9.

Row 14: Turn (do not ch1), sc dec (see Notes), sc30 (31 sts).

Row 15: Turn, ch1, sc31 (31 sts).

Row 16: Turn, sc dec, sc29 (30 sts).

Row 17: Turn, ch1, sc28, sc dec (29 sts).

Row 18: Turn, sc dec, sc27 (28 sts).

Row 19: Turn, ch1, sc26, sc dec (27 sts).

Row 20: Turn, sc dec, sc25 (26 sts).

Row 21: Turn, ch1, sc24, sc dec (25 sts).

Rows 22–27: Turn, ch1, sc25 (25 sts).

Row 28: Turn, ch1, 2sc in first stitch, sc24 (26 sts).

Row 29: Turn, ch1, sc25, 2sc in last stitch (27 sts).

Row 30: Turn, ch1, 2sc in first stitch, sc26 (28 sts).

Row 31: Turn, ch1, sc27, 2sc in last stitch (29 sts) **Row 32:** Turn, ch1, 2sc in first stitch, sc28 (30 sts).

Row 33: Turn, ch1, sc29, 2sc in last stitch (31 sts).

Row 34: Turn, ch1, sc31 (31 sts).

Row 35: Turn, ch1, 2sc in first stitch, sc30 (32 sts).

Rows 36–40: Turn, ch1, sc32 (32 sts).

Row 41: Turn, ch1, sc24 (24 sts) **Row 42:** Turn, sc dec, sc23 (23 sts).

Row 43: Turn, ch1, sc21, sc dec (22 sts).

Row 44: Turn, sc dec, sc20 (21 sts).

Row 45: Turn, ch1, sc19, sc dec (20 sts).

Row 46: Turn, sc dec, sc18 (19 sts).

Row 47: Turn, ch1, sc17, sc dec (18 sts).

Row 48: Turn, ch1, sc18 (18 sts). (Front panel complete.) **Row 49:** Turn, ch1, sc17, 2sc in last stitch (19 sts).

Row 50: Turn, ch1, 2sc in first stitch, sc18 (20 sts).
Row 51: Turn, ch1, sc19, 2sc in last stitch (21 sts).
Row 52: Turn, ch1, 2sc in first stitch, sc20 (22 sts).
Row 53: Turn, ch1, sc21, 2sc in last stitch (23 sts).
Row 54: Turn, ch1, 2sc in first stitch, sc22 (24 sts).
Row 55: Turn, ch1, sc24, ch15 (39 sts).
Row 56: Turn, sc in first chain from hook and across (38 sts).
Row 57: Turn, sc34, ch2, skip 2 stitches, sc2 (38 sts).
Row 58: Turn, ch1, sc38 (38 sts).
Row 59: Turn, sc34, ch2, skip 2 stitches, sc2 (38 sts).
Row 60: Turn, ch1, sc38 (38 sts).
Row 61: Turn, ch1, sc32 (32 sts).
Row 62: Turn, sc dec, sc30 (31 sts).
Row 63: Turn, ch1, sc29, sc dec (30 sts).
Row 64: Turn, sc dec, sc28 (29 sts).
Row 65: Turn, ch1, sc27, sc dec (28 sts).
Rows 66–80: Turn, ch1, sc28 (28 sts).
Row 81: Turn, ch1, sc27, 2sc in last stitch (29 sts).
Row 82: Turn, ch1, 2sc in first stitch, sc28 (30 sts).
Row 83: Turn, ch1, sc29, 2sc in last stitch (31 sts).
Row 84: Turn, ch1, 2sc in first stitch, sc30 (32 sts).
Row 85: Turn, ch1, sc32, ch7 (39 sts).
Row 86: Turn, sc in first chain from hook and across (38 sts).
Row 87: Turn, ch1, sc34, ch2, skip 2 stitches, sc2 (38 sts).
Row 88: Turn, ch1, sc38 (38 sts).
Row 89: Turn, ch1, sc34, ch1, skip 2 stitches, sc2 (38 sts).
Row 90: Turn, ch1, sc38 (38 sts).
Row 91: Turn, ch1, sc24 (24 sts) **Row 92:** Turn, sc dec, sc22 (23 sts).
Row 93: Turn, ch1, sc21, sc dec (22 sts).
Row 94: Turn, sc dec sc20 (21 sts).
Row 95: Turn, ch1, sc19, sc dec (20 sts).
Row 96: Turn, sc dec, sc18 (19 sts).
Row 97: Turn, ch1, sc17, sc dec (18 sts).
Row 98: Turn, ch1, sc18 (18 sts).
Fasten off, leaving a long tail to sew the side seam.
Using the yarn needle, whipstitch the sides together. Do not sew the shoulders.

Bottom Edging

With right side facing out, join Color B at seam.

Round 1: Ch1, using the ends of rows as stitches, sl st in each stitch around. Sl st to ch1 to join (98 sts).

Round 2: Ch1, *using blo (see Notes), sl st in next 3 stitches, sl st dec (see Special Technique on page 25), repeat from * until 3 stitches remain in round. Sl st in blo of remaining stitches to complete round, sl st to ch1 to join round (60 sts).

Round 3: Ch1, sl st in blo of each stitch, sl st to ch1 to join round (60 sts).

Fasten off Color B, join Color C.

Round 4: Ch1, sl st in both loops of each stitch, sl st to ch1 to join round (60 sts).

Fasten off. Weave in ends.

Top Edging

With right side facing out, join Color B at seam.

Round 1: Ch1, using ends of rows as stitches, sl st in each stitch around, with the exception of the 4 corners of the shoulder straps. In each corner of straps, (sl st, ch1, sl st) in that stitch. Sl st to ch1 to join round.

Round 2: Ch1, sl st in blo of each stitch around, with the exception of the corners of the shoulder straps. In the corners, (sl st, ch1, sl st) in previous ch1 space. Sl st to join round.

Fasten off Color B, join Color C.

Round 3: Ch1, sl st in both loops of each stitch around, with the exception of the corners of the shoulder straps. In the corners, (sl st, ch1, sl st) in previous ch1 space. Sl st to join round.

Fasten off. Weave in ends.

With sewing needle and thread, sew buttons onto front of vest and slip straps over. Vest is complete.

Tie

Using Color C, ch9.

Row 1: Turn, sc in first chain from hook and across (8 sts).

Row 2: Turn, sc dec, sc4, sc dec (6 sts).

Row 3: Turn, sc dec, sc2, sc dec (4 sts).

Row 4: Turn, sc dec, sc dec (2 sts).

Row 5: Turn, ch1, 2sc in each stitch (4 sts).
Row 6: Turn, ch1, 2sc in first stitch, sc2, 2sc in last stitch (6 sts).
Row 7: Turn, ch1, sc6 (6 sts).
Row 8: Turn, ch1, 2sc in first stitch, sc4, 2sc in last stitch (8 sts).
Rows 9–17: Turn, ch1, sc8 (8 sts).
Row 18: Turn, sc dec, sc4, sc dec (6 sts).
Row 19: Turn, sc dec, sc2, sc dec (4 sts).
Row 20: Turn, sc dec, sc dec (2 sts).
Row 21: Turn, sc dec, ch1.

Fasten off, leaving a long tail to sew the tie onto the vest.

With the yarn needle, sew along the edges of the tie to secure it to the vest. Fasten off.

Using Color B, sl st the tie clip as an embellishment on top of the tie. Fasten off. Weave in all ends.

Every little girl needs a hat that can be worn each season, and this is it. Make it in a variety of colors to complete your little girl's accessory wardrobe.

Finished Measurements

6–12 months: Circumference, 18"; Hat height, 6"

(For other sizes, see Notes.) **Yarn**

- Caron Sheep(ish) by Vickie Howell, medium worsted weight #4 yarn, 70% acrylic/30% wool (167 yd/3 oz per skein)
  - 1 skein #7 Turquoise(ish) (Color A)
  - 1 skein #17 Pink(ish) (Color B)

Hook and Other Materials

• K-6.5mm hook or size needed to obtain gauge
• Yarn needle

Gauge
11 sts and 14 rows in sc = 3" square

Notes

1. The hat is worked from the top down in the round.
2. The first ch3 of each round counts as a dc throughout the pattern.
3. The size can be made smaller or larger by using a smaller or larger hook to decrease or increase gauge.

Special Technique

Cluster

4dc, sl st to first dc. The sl st will join the 4 stitches into 1 stitch, creating a cluster.

Hat

Using Color A, ch4, sl st to first chain to create a ring.

Round 1: Ch3 (counts as first dc here and throughout), 3dc in ring, sl st to third chain of ch3 to make first cluster, ch3, cluster (see Special Technique), ch3, cluster, ch3, cluster, ch3, sl st to third chain of first ch3 to join round (16 sts).

Round 2: Ch3, 3dc in last ch3 space of previous round, sl st to third chain of first ch3 to make first cluster, *ch3, (cluster, ch3, cluster) in next ch3 space from previous round. Repeat from* to last ch3 space. To finish, ch3, sl st to third chain of first ch3 (8 clusters and 8 ch3 spaces created for a total of 32 sts).

Round 3: Ch3, 3dc in last ch3 space of previous round, sl st to third chain of first ch3 to make first cluster, *ch3, (cluster, ch3, cluster) in next ch3 space from previous round, repeat from* to last ch3 space. To finish, ch3, sl st to third chain of first ch3 (16 clusters and 16 ch3 spaces created for a total of 64 sts).

Round 4: Ch3, 3dc in last ch3 space of previous round, sl st to third chain of first ch3 to make first cluster, *ch1, cluster in ch3 space of previous round, ch1, cluster in ch3 space of previous round, repeat from* to complete round, ch1, sl st to third chain of first ch3 to join (32 sts).

Round 5: Ch3, 3dc in last ch1 space of previous round, sl st to third chain of first ch3 to make first cluster, *ch1, cluster in ch1 space of previous round, ch1, cluster in ch1 space of previous round, repeat from* to complete round, ch1, sl st to third chain of first ch3 to join (32 sts).

Rounds 6–8: Repeat Round 5.

Round 9: Ch1, sc in each stitch (32 sts).

Round 10–13: Working continuously in the round, repeat Round 9. To finish, sl st to first stitch of round.

Fasten off. Weave in ends.

Flowers

Top Flower

Using Color B, ch4, sl st to first chain to create a ring.

Round 1: Ch1, 5sc in ring, do not join (5 sts).

Round 2: Sl st to first stitch. In same stitch (ch1, hdc, dc, tr, dc, hdc, ch1, sl st), *sl st to next stitch and in same stitch (ch1, hdc, dc, tr, dc, hdc, ch1, sl st), repeat from* to complete 5 petals.

To finish, sl st to first ch1 to complete first level.

Do not fasten off; work straight into Middle Flower.

Middle Flower

Round 1: Ch1, 5sc in ring, do not join (5 sts).

Round 2: Sl st to first stitch. In same stitch (ch1, hdc, dc, tr, dc, hdc, ch1, sl st), *sl st to next stitch and in same stitch (ch1, hdc, dc, tr, dc, hdc, ch1, sl st), repeat from* to complete 5 petals.

Round 3: *Ch3, sl st to slip stitch created in between the petals, repeat from* around the flower. It can be in front of the petals, because it will form correctly and lie flat when finished. After completing the 5 ch3 sections, work right into the petals.

Round 4: Sl st to first ch3 space, work (ch1, hdc, dc, tr, dc, hdc, ch1, sl st) in space, *sl st to next ch3 space, work (ch1, hdc, dc, tr, dc, hdc, ch1, sl st) in space, repeat from* to complete 5 petals.

To finish, sl st to first ch1.

Do not fasten off; work straight into Back Flower.

Back Flower

Repeat Middle Flower.

Fasten off. Weave in ends.

Arrange flower levels on top of one another so that the petals all lie correctly and are not hidden behind the others. Attach the flower with yarn needle to hat.

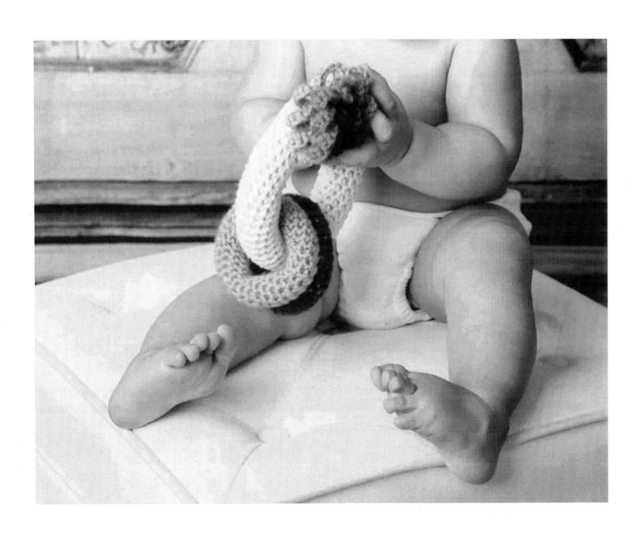

The Love Me Lots Toy is a great scrap buster project for a baby gift or small toy. And best of all, you can say that you made it!

Finished Measurements
Main tube: 18"
Small tubes: 10"

Yarn

- Lion Brand Vanna's Choice Baby, medium worsted weight #4 yarn, 100% acrylic (170 yd/3.5 oz per skein)

  1 skein #840-098 Lamb (Color A)

- Lion Brand Vanna's Choice, medium worsted weight #4 yarn, 100% acrylic (170 yd/3.5 oz per skein)

  1 skein #860-140 Dusty Rose (Color B)

  1 skein #860-143 Antique Rose (Color C)

  1 skein #860-125 Taupe (Color D)

Hook and Other Materials

- F-3.75mm hook
- Stitch marker (optional)
- Yarn needle
- Fiberfill

Gauge

11 sts and 10 rows in sc = 3" square (exact gauge not important) **Notes**

1. Make all of the tubes first. Sew the smaller ones together, slip over the main tube, and then sew the main tube together. The optional flowers are added last.
2. For boys, add stripes in the main tube and more rings as preferred. The flowers are optional; use any color combination to make them.
3. To make the small tubes larger and different sizes, add extra rows until the desired length is reached.
4. Tubes are worked continuously in the round. If you like, mark the first stitch of the round with a stitch marker for reference.
5. See page 121 for a tutorial on how to whipstitch seams.

Main Tube

Using Color A, ch15, sl st to first chain to create a ring.

Round 1: Ch1, sc in each chain, do not join (15 sts).

Rounds 2–65: Working continuously in the round, sc in each stitch (15 sts). To finish, sl st to first sc of next round.

Fasten off, leaving a long tail to sew ends together. Do not sew together until directed. Stuff with fiberfill.

Small Tubes (make 2–4 using Colors B, C, D)

Ch8, sl st to first chain to create a ring.

Round 1: Ch1, sc in each chain, do not join (8 sts).

Rounds 2–35: Working continuously in the round, sc in each stitch (8 sts). To finish, sl st to first sc of next round.

Fasten off, leaving a long tail to sew together. Stuff tubes with fiberfill. Whipstitch the ends together to finish (see Notes). Weave in ends.

Slip the long tube through the smaller rings. Whipstitch the ends of the long tube together. Weave in ends.

Flowers

Back Flower (optional)

Ch4, sl st to first chain to create a ring.

Round 1: Ch1, 10sc in ring, sl st to first sc (not ch1) to join (10 sts).

Round 2: Ch8, sl st to same stitch, *in next stitch (sl st, ch8, sl st), repeat from* in each stitch (10 petals).

Round 3: Sc10 in first ch8 space, *sl st to next ch8 space, sc10 in loop, repeat from* to complete each petal. To finish, sl st to first sc of Round 1 to join.

Fasten off. Weave in ends.

Middle Flower (optional)

Ch4, sl st to first chain to create a ring.

Round 1: Ch1, 10sc in ring, sl st to first sc (not ch1) to join (10 sts).

Round 2: Ch6, sl st to same stitch, *in next stitch (sl st, ch6, sl st), repeat from* in each stitch (10 petals).

Round 3: Sc8 in first ch8 space, *sl st to next ch6 space, sc8 in loop, repeat from* to complete each petal. To finish, sl st to first sc of Round 1 to join.

Fasten off. Weave in ends.

Top Flower (optional)

Ch4, sl st to first chain to create a ring.

Round 1: Ch1, 6sc in ring, sl st to first sc (not ch1) to join (10 sts).

Round 2: Ch2, sl st to same stitch, *in next stitch (sl st, ch2, sl st), repeat from* in each stitch (10 petals).

Round 3: Sc4 in first ch2 space, *sl st to next ch2 space, sc4 in loop, repeat from* to complete each petal. To finish, sl st to first sc of Round 1 to join.

Fasten off. Weave in ends.

Finishing

With yarn needle, sew the 3 flowers together using the middle ring and then attach to the top of the seam of the main tube to finish. Weave in ends.

Double your baby's cuteness with this sweet and simple double pom hat!

Finished Measurements Newborn: Circumference, 12–14";
　　Hat height, 4.5"
3–6 months: Circumference, 14–17";
　　Hat height, 6"
9–12 months: Circumference, 16–19";
　　Hat height, 7.5"

Yarn
- Lion Brand Vanna's Choice, medium worsted weight #4 yarn, 100% acrylic (170 yd/3.5 oz per skein)
    - 1 skein #860-302 Taupe Mist (Color A)
- Lion Brand Vanna's Choice Baby, medium worsted weight #4 yarn, 100% acrylic (170 yd/3.5 oz per skein)
    - 1 skein #860-143 Antique Rose (Color B)

Hook and Other Materials • G-4.25mm hook or size needed to obtain gauge • Stitch marker (optional)

Gauge
12 sts and 13 rows in sc = 3" square

Notes
1. The hat is worked from the bottom up.
2. For the portion of the hat that is worked continuously in the round, if you like, mark the first stitch of the round with a stitch marker for reference.
3. See page 113 for a tutorial on Front Post Double Crochet (fpdc), page 114 for Back Post Double Crochet (bpdc), page 107 for how to crochet into a back loop only (blo), and page 120 for how to make poms.

Hat

Newborn

Using Color A, ch44, sl st to first chain to create a ring.

Round 1: Ch1, sc in each stitch, sl st to ch1 to join (44 sts).

Rounds 2–5: Ch3, *fpdc3 (see Notes), bpdc (see Notes), repeat from * to complete round, sl st to ch3 to join (44 sts).

Fasten off Color A; join Color B.

Round 6: Ch1, sc in blo (see Notes) in each stitch (44 sts).

Rounds 7–20: Working continuously in the round, sc in each stitch, sl st to first stitch of round to finish (44 sts).

Fasten off, leaving a long tail to sew the top together.

3–6 Months

Using Color A, ch52, sl st to first chain to create a ring.

Round 1: Ch1, sc in each stitch, sl st to ch1 to join (52 sts).

Rounds 2–7: Ch3, *fpdc3 (see Notes), bpdc (see Notes), repeat from * to complete round, sl st to ch3 to join (52 sts).

Fasten off Color A; join Color B.

Round 8: Ch1, sc in blo (see Notes) in each stitch (52 sts).

Rounds 9–24: Working continuously in the round, sc in each stitch, sl st to first stitch of round to finish (52 sts).

Fasten off, leaving a long tail to sew the top together.

9–12 Months

Using Color A, ch60, sl st to first chain to create a ring.

Round 1: Ch1, sc in each stitch, sl st to ch1 to join (60 sts).

Rounds 2–7: Ch3, *fpdc3 (see Notes), bpdc (see Notes), repeat from * to complete round, sl st to ch3 to join (60 sts).

Fasten off Color A; join Color B.

Round 8: Ch1, sc in blo (see Notes) in each stitch (60 sts).

Rounds 9–30: Working continuously in the round, sc in each stitch, sl st to first stitch of round to finish (60 sts).

Fasten off, leaving a long tail to sew the top together.

Finishing

With yarn needle, sew top of hat together.

Create 2 poms in Color A (see Notes) and attach to the top corners of the hat.

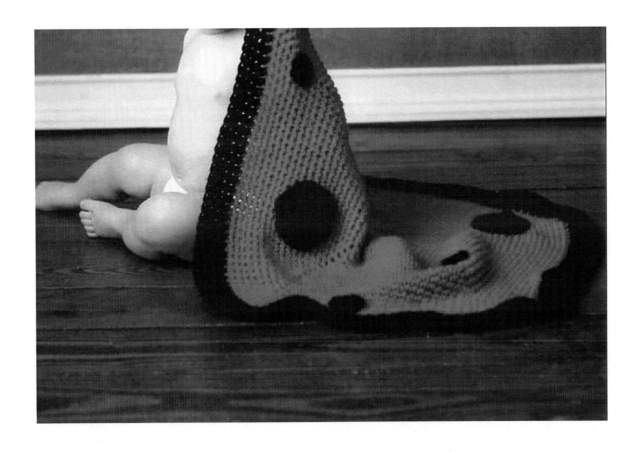

This one-of-a-kind blanket is perfect to wrap your little ladybug in for trips to the store, a visit to Grandma's house, or a ride in the park.

Finished Measurements

Hood: Width, 15"; Height, 5.5"

Blanket: 30" in diameter

(To adjust size, see Notes.) **Yarn**

- Yarn Bee I Love This Yarn!, medium worsted weight #4 yarn, 100% acrylic (355 yd/7 oz per skein)

       1 skein #40 Red (Color A)

       1 skein #30 Black (Color B)

Hook and Other Materials
- H-5.0mm hook or size needed to obtain gauge
- N-9.0mm hook or size needed to obtain gauge
- Yarn needle

Gauge

Using H-5.0mm hook, 16 sts and 14 rows in sc = 4" square Using N-9.0mm hook, 12 sts and 11 rows in sc = 4" square **Notes**

1. The blanket is made in 2 sections. The hood is crocheted directly onto the blanket.
2. The N-9.0mm hook will be used for the blanket and the 5.0mm will be used for the hood and spots.
3. From Round 2, the blanket is worked continuously in the round. If you like, mark the first stitch of the round with a stitch marker for reference.
4. To extend the width of the hood, increase by multiples of 5 stitches and 5 rows (example: if you increase the length by 10 stitches, add 10 rows).
5. You can increase or decrease the number of spots in the different sizes as you prefer.

Blanket

Using Color A and N-9.0mm hook, ch4, sl st to first chain to create a ring.
Round 1: 8sc in ring, do not join (8 sts).
Round 2: Working continuously in the round, 2sc in each stitch (16 sts).
Round 3: *Sc, 2sc in next stitch, repeat from* to complete round (24 sts).
Round 4: *Sc2, 2sc in next stitch, repeat from* to complete round (32 sts).

Round 5: *Sc3, 2sc in next stitch, repeat from* to complete round (40 sts).
Round 6: *Sc4, 2sc in next stitch, repeat from* to complete round (48 sts).
Round 7: *Sc5, 2sc in next stitch, repeat from* to complete round (56 sts).
Round 8: *Sc6, 2sc in next stitch, repeat from* to complete round (64 sts).
Round 9: *Sc7, 2sc in next stitch, repeat from* to complete round (72 sts).
Round 10: *Sc8, 2sc in next stitch, repeat from* to complete round (80 sts).
Round 11: *Sc9, 2sc in next stitch, repeat from* to complete round (88 sts).
Round 12: *Sc10, 2sc in next stitch, repeat from* to complete round (96 sts).
Round 13: *Sc11, 2sc in next stitch, repeat from* to complete round (104 sts).
Round 14: *Sc12, 2sc in next stitch, repeat from* to complete round (112 sts).
Round 15: *Sc13, 2sc in next stitch, repeat from* to complete round (120 sts).
Round 16: *Sc14, 2sc in next stitch, repeat from* to complete round (128 sts).
Round 17: *Sc15, 2sc in next stitch, repeat from* to complete round (136 sts).
Round 18: *Sc16, 2sc in next stitch, repeat from* to complete round (144 sts).
Round 19: *Sc17, 2sc in next stitch, repeat from* to complete round (152 sts).
Round 20: *Sc18, 2sc in next stitch, repeat from* to complete round (160 sts).
Round 21: *Sc19, 2sc in next stitch, repeat from* to complete round (168 sts).

Round 22: *Sc20, 2sc in next stitch, repeat from* to complete round (176 sts).
Round 23: *Sc21, 2sc in next stitch, repeat from* to complete round (184 sts).
Round 24: *Sc22, 2sc in next stitch, repeat from* to complete round (192 sts).
Fasten off Color A, join Color B.
Round 25: *Sc23, 2sc in next stitch, repeat from* to complete round (200 sts).
Round 26: *Sc24, 2sc in next stitch, repeat from* to complete round (208 sts).
Round 27: *Sc25, 2sc in next stitch, repeat from* to complete round (216 sts).
Round 28: *Sc26, 2sc in next stitch, repeat from* to complete round, sl st to first stitch of round to finish (224 sts).
Fasten off Color B.

Hood

Using H-5.0mm hook, join Color A in any stitch at outer edge of blanket.
Row 1: Sc38.
Rows 2–30: Turn, ch1, sc38.
Fasten off, leaving a long tail to sew the top together.
Using yarn needle, sew the top together to create the hood.

Hood Trim

Join Color A with a sl st to bottom left corner of hood.
Using ends of rows as stitches, ch1, *skip 1 stitch, sl st to next stitch, skip 1 stitch, 5dc in next stitch, repeat from* to where the other side of the hood meets the blanket. Sl st to last stitch to finish.
Fasten off. Weave in ends

Spots

Use Color B and H-5.0mm hook.

Small

Round 1: Ch2, 4sc in first chain (4 sts).

Round 2: 2sc in each stitch, sl st to first stitch of round to join (8 sts).

Fasten off, leaving a long tail to sew onto the blanket.

Medium

Round 1: Ch2, 6sc in first chain (6 sts).

Round 2: Working continuously in the round, 2sc in each stitch (12 sts).

Round 3: *Sc, 2sc in next stitch, repeat from* to complete round, sl st to first stitch of round to join (18 sts).

Fasten off, leaving a long tail to sew onto the blanket.

Large

Round 1: Ch2, 6sc in first chain (6 sts).

Round 2: Working continuously in the round, 2sc in each stitch (12 sts).

Round 3: *Sc, 2sc in next stitch, repeat from* to complete round (18 sts).

Round 4: *Sc2, 2sc in next stitch, repeat from* to complete round (24 sts).

Round 5: *Sc3, 2sc in next stitch, repeat from* to complete round, sl st to first stitch of round to join (30 sts).

Fasten off, leaving a long tail to sew onto the blanket.

Using the yarn needle, sew each spot randomly onto the blanket and hood.

Weave in ends Antennas (make 2)

Using Color B and H-5.0mm hook, ch40.

Row 1: Turn, 3sc in each chain.

Fasten off, leaving a long tail to sew onto the hood.

Using the yarn needle, sew the ends of the antennas onto the hood. Weave in ends.

Dress up any outfit with this simple headband. You'll be amazed at how fast you'll make this sweet accessory . . . and how easy the flowers are!

Finished Measurements Newborn: Circumference, 12–14"
3–6 months: Circumference, 14–15"
6–9 months: Circumference, 15–17"
9–12 months: Circumference, 16–19"

Yarn

• Yarn Bee I Love This Cotton!, medium worsted weight #4 yarn, 100% cotton
  (180 yd/3.5 oz per skein)
  > 1 skein #24 Ivory (Color A)
  > 1 skein #48 Taupe (Color B)
  > 1 skein #20 Brown (Color C)

Hook and Other Materials • F-3.75mm hook or size needed to obtain gauge • J-6mm hook
• N-9mm hook
• Yarn needle

Gauge

Using F-3.75mm hook, 18 sts and 15 rows in sc = 3" square **Notes**

1. The headband is made in 1 strip, sewn together, and the flower added over the seam to make it appear seamless.
2. The flowers are very easy to make. Even though they are 3 different sizes, they use the same pattern; what changes is the size hook you use to make each one.

Headband

Newborn

Using Color A, ch39.

Row 1: Turn, hdc in first chain from hook and across (38 sts).

Row 2: Turn, ch1, *skip 2 stitches, 5dc in next stitch, repeat from* to 3 stitches from end of row, skip 2 stitches, sl st in last stitch (37 sts). Fasten off.

Row 3: Turn piece so Row 2 is on the bottom. Join Color A to top right unworked stitch. Ch1, *skip 2 stitches, 5dc in next stitch, repeat from* to 3 stitches from end of row, skip 2 stitches, sl st in last stitch (37 sts).

Fasten off. With yarn needle, sew the ends together. Weave in ends.

3–6 Months

Using Color A, ch45.

Row 1: Turn, hdc in first chain from hook and across (44 sts).

Row 2: Turn, ch1, *skip 2 stitches, 5dc in next stitch, repeat from* to 3 stitches from end of row, skip 2 stitches, sl st in last stitch (43 sts). Fasten off.

Row 3: Turn piece so Row 2 is on the bottom. Join Color A to top right unworked stitch. Ch1, *skip 2 stitches, 5dc in next stitch, repeat from* to 3 stitches from end of row, skip 2 stitches, sl st in last stitch (43 sts).

Fasten off. With yarn needle, sew the ends together. Weave in ends.

6–9 Months

Using Color A, ch51.

Row 1: Turn, hdc in first chain from hook and across (50 sts).

Row 2: Turn, ch1, *skip 2 stitches, 5dc in next stitch, repeat from* to 3 stitches from end of row, skip 2 stitches, sl st in last stitch (49 sts). Fasten off.

Row 3: Turn piece so Row 2 is on the bottom. Join Color A at top right unworked stitch. Ch1, *skip 2 stitches, 5dc in next stitch, repeat from* to 3 stitches from end of row, skip 2 stitches, sl st in last stitch (49 sts).

Fasten off. With yarn needle, sew the ends together. Weave in ends.

9–12 Months

Using Color A, ch57.

Row 1: Turn, hdc in first chain from hook and across (56 sts).

Row 2: Turn, ch1, *skip 2 stitches, 5dc in next stitch, repeat from* to 3 stitches from end of row, skip 2 stitches, sl st in last stitch (55 sts). Fasten off.

Row 3: Turn piece so Row 2 is on the bottom. Join Color A at top right unworked stitch. Ch1, *skip 2 stitches, 5dc in next stitch, repeat from* to 3 stitches from end of row, skip 2 stitches, sl st in last stitch (55 sts).

Fasten off. With yarn needle, sew the ends together. Weave in ends.

Flowers (make 3)

Back flower: Use Color B and N-9mm hook.

Middle flower: Use Color A and J-6mm hook.

Top flower: Use Color C and F-3.75 hook.

Ch4, sl st to first chain to join.

Round 1: Ch1, 6sc in ring, sl st to first chain to create a ring (6 sts).

Round 2: Ch1, *sl st to next stitch, (ch1, 2dc, ch1) and sl st to same stitch, repeat from* in each stitch to complete round, sl st to ch1 to join (6 petals).

Fasten off. Weave in ends

Center of Flower

Using Color B and F-3.75mm hook, ch2.
Round 1: 6sc in first chain, sl st to first chain to create a ring (6sc).
Pull center tight. Fasten off. Weave in ends.

Finishing

With yarn needle, sew the flower stack together in the middle of the ring. Sew the center on top of the flower stack. Sew the flower stack on top of the headband seam. Fasten off. Weave in ends.

I love to mix yarns to create wonderful textures. Using basic stitches, you can crochet a stunning accessory that will amaze you and your friends.

Finished Measurements

Newborn: Circumference, 12–14"; Hat height, 5.5–6"
3–6 months: Circumference, 14–17"; Hat height, 6.5–7"
9–12 months: Circumference, 16–19"; Hat height, 7.5"

Yarn

- Bernat Giggles, medium worsted weight #4 yarn, 90% acrylic/10% nylon (185 yd/3.5 oz per skein)
    1 skein #56510 Cheery Cream (Color A)
- Heartstrings by Dee Thick and Thin (*HeartstringsbyDee.etsy.com*), super bulky #6 yarn, 100% merino (15 yd/1.5 oz per skein)
    1 skein Rusty Peach Colorway (Color B)

Hook and Other Materials
- H-5.0mm hook or size needed to obtain gauge
- Stitch marker (optional)
- Yarn needle

Gauge

Using Color A, 14 sts and 16 rows in sc = 4" square **Notes**

1. The hat is worked from the bottom up continuously in the round. If you like, mark the first stitch of each round with a stitch marker for reference.
2. When using the Thick and Thin yarn, work loosely so that the texture stays intact. If the yarn is pulled tight, the texture will not be seen.
3. When you change from Color A to Color B, you will carry Color A, not fasten it off. That will allow you to simply pick the yarn up later, with no ends to weave in. For a tutorial, see page 117. (Because of its thickness, Color B is too difficult to carry, so it gets fastened off each time.) 4. See page 119 for a tutorial on how to make tassels.

Hat

Newborn

Using Color A, ch39.

Round 1: Sc in first chain and in each ch around, sl st to first chain to create a ring (38 sts).

Round 2: Ch1, sc in each stitch around; do not join (38 sts).

Rounds 3–6: Working continuously in the round, sc in each stitch (38 sts).

Drop Color A (see Notes), join Color B.

Round 7: *Sc, dc, repeat from* to complete round (38 sts).

Fasten off Color B, pick up Color A.

Rounds 8–9: Sc in each stitch (38 sts).

Round 10: Repeat Round 7.

Drop Color A, join Color B.

Rounds 11–17: Sc in each stitch (38 sts). To finish, sl st to first stitch of round.

Fasten off, leaving a long tail to sew top together.

Using yarn needle, sew the top together.

3–6 Months

Using Color A, ch45.

Round 1: Sc in first chain and in each ch around, sl st to first chain to create a ring (44 sts).

Round 2: Ch1, sc in each stitch to complete round, do not join (44 sts).

Rounds 3–6: Working continuously in the round, sc in each stitch (44 sts).

Drop Color A (see Notes), join Color B.

Round 7: *Sc, dc, repeat from* to complete round (44 sts).
Fasten off Color B, pick up Color A.
Rounds 8–9: Sc in each stitch (44 sts).
Round 10: Repeat Round 7.
Drop Color A, join Color B.
Rounds 11–20: Sc in each stitch (44 sts). To finish, sl st to first stitch of round.
Fasten off, leaving a long tail to sew top together.
Using yarn needle, sew the top together.

9–12 Months

Using Color A, ch51.
Round 1: Sc in first chain and in each ch around, sl st to first chain to create a
    ring (50 sts).
Round 2: Ch1, sc in each stitch to complete round; do not join (50 sts).
Rounds 3–8: Working continuously in the round, sc in each stitch (50 sts).
Drop Color A, join Color B.
Round 9: *Sc, dc, repeat from* to complete round (50 sts).
Fasten off Color B, pick up Color A.
Rounds 10–11 Sc in each stitch (50 sts).
Round 12: Repeat Round 9.
Drop Color A, join Color B.
Rounds 13–25: Sc in each stitch (50 sts). To finish, sl st to first stitch of round.
Fasten off, leaving a long tail to sew top together.
Using yarn needle, sew top together.

Tassels (make 2)

Make 2 tassels using Color A (see Notes). Tie the tassels to the corners of the hat.

Keep your little sweet pea warm and cozy in this adorable peapod. Not only is it the cutest personal blanket, but it's also the best shower gift you can make.

Finished Measurements

Newborn
Length: 19.5"; Circumference: 16"

Yarn

- Red Heart Super Saver, medium worsted weight #4 yarn, 100% acrylic (364 yd/7 oz per skein)
    1 skein in #0624 Tea Leaf

Hook and Other Materials
• H-5.0mm hook or size needed to obtain gauge • Stitch marker (optional)
• Yarn needle

Gauge

12 sts and 13 rows in sc = 4" square

Notes
1. The cocoon works right into the hood in 1 continuous piece.
2. The base is worked continuously in rounds and the hood is worked in rows.
3. If you like, mark the first stitch of the round with a stitch marker for reference.

Cocoon

Ch4, sl st to first chain to create a ring.
Round 1: Ch1 (this counts as your first sc), 7sc in ring (8 sts).
Round 2: Working continuously in the round, 2sc in each stitch (16 sts).
Round 3: *Sc, 2sc in next stitch, repeat from* to complete round (24 sts).
Round 4: *Sc2, 2sc in next stitch, repeat from* to complete round (32 sts).
Round 5: *Sc3, 2sc in next stitch, repeat from* to complete round (40 sts).
Round 6: *Sc4, 2sc in next stitch, repeat from* to complete round (48 sts).
Round 7: *Sc5, 2sc in next stitch, repeat from* to complete round (56 sts).
Round 8: *Sc6, 2sc in next stitch, repeat from* to complete round (64 sts).
Rounds 9–56: Sc in each stitch (64 sts).
Row 57: Turn, ch1, sc48 (48 sts).
Rows 58–77: Repeat Row 57.
Fasten off, leaving a long tail of yarn.
Fold the top with the 2 corners touching, and with the yarn needle, sew together
   with a whipstitch using the long tail to create the hood. Weave in ends.

When sewing the top, start at the edges and work to the back. Fasten off and
weave in ends.

Trim

Round 1: Join yarn at edge of top seam, ch1, sc around using ends of rows as stitches, sl st to ch1 to join.

Round 2: Ch1, sc in each stitch to complete round, sl st to ch1 to join.

Fasten off. Weave in ends.

Peapod Tendrils (make 3)

Ch25.

Row 1: 3sc in each chain.

Fasten off.

Attach curls to top of the hood by knotting to inside of back of hood.

Throw all your boring bibs out and replace them with this adorable hippo bib. With its perky ears and toothy grin, it will be the talk of all meals.

Finished Measurements

7" x 7"

Yarn

- Peaches & Crème, medium worsted weight #4 yarn, 100% cotton (98 yd/2.0 oz. per skein)
    - 1 skein Orchid (Color A)
    - 1 skein Ecru (Color B)
    - 1 skein Bright Pink (Color C)
    - 1 skein White (Color D)
    - 1 skein Black (Color E)

Hook and Other Materials
- H-5.0mm hook or size needed to obtain gauge
- Yarn needle

Gauge
10 sts and 8 rows in hdc = 3" square

Notes
1. The bib base is worked from the bottom to the top.
2. Color A can be changed to any color to make the bib gender specific.
3. The ties are secured to the bib base with single crochet.
4. See page 110 for a tutorial on Half Double Crochet (hdc), page 110 for Half Double Crochet Decrease (hdc dec), page 109 for Single Crochet Decrease (sc dec), and page 107 for how to work through the front loop only (flo) of a stitch.

Bib Base

Using Color A, ch23.

Row 1: Hdc in second chain from hook and in each chain across (22 sts).

Row 2: Turn, ch2, hdc in first stitch and across (22 sts).

Rows 3–12: Repeat Row 2.

Row 13: Turn, hdc dec (see Notes), hdc18, hdc dec using last 2 stitches (20 sts).

Row 14: Turn, hdc dec, hdc16, hdc dec using last 2 stitches (18 sts).

Row 15: Turn, hdc dec, hdc14, hdc dec using last 2 stitches (16 sts).

Row 16: Turn, hdc dec, hdc12, hdc dec using last 2 stitches (14 sts).

Row 17: Turn, hdc dec, hdc10, hdc dec using last 2 stitches (12 sts).

Fasten off Color A. Join Color B

Row 18: Turn, ch1, sc in first stitch and across (12 sts).

Do not fasten off.

Bib Trim

Using ends of rows as stitches, with Color B sc down first side of bib base, 3sc
    in the corner, sc across bottom, and 3sc in next corner. Using ends of rows as
    stitches, sc up third side, and join trim row with a sl st to first stitch of Row
    18.

Fasten off. Weave in ends.

Nose

With right side up and the bottom of the bib closest to you, locate the second sc in the 3sc set in bottom right corner.

Row 1: Join Color B, ch1, sc in each stitch through flo (see Notes) to end of row (24 sts).

Row 2: Turn, ch1, sc in each stitch through both loops to end of row (24 sts).

Row 3: Turn, sc dec, sc20, sc dec using last 2 stitches (22 sts).

Row 4: Turn, sc dec, sc18, sc dec using last 2 stitches (20 sts).

Row 5: Turn, sc dec, sc16, sc dec using last 2 stitches (18 sts).

Row 6: Turn, sc dec, sc14, sc dec using last 2 stitches (16 sts).

Row 7: Turn, sc dec, sc12, sc dec using last 2 stitches (14 sts).

Fasten off.

Fold nose up onto bib. Starting at bottom right corner of nose, join Color B, using ends of rows as stitches, sc around the nose to trim.

Fasten off, leaving a long tail. Sew the nose onto the bib with yarn needle.

Cheeks (make 2)

Using Color C, ch2.

Row 1: 6sc in first chain, sl st to first stitch.

Fasten off, leaving a long tail. Sew cheeks onto the "corners" of nose.

Ears (make 2)

Using Color A, ch5.

Row 1: Turn, sc first chain from hook and across (4 sts).

Row 2: Turn, sc3, 2sc in last stitch (5 sts).

Row 3: Working on the opposite side of chain, 2sc in next stitch, sc to end of row.

Fasten off, leaving a long tail. Sew onto front of the bib 3 stitches in from both ends of Row 16.

Eyes (make 2)

Using Color D, ch2.

Round 1: 8sc in first chain.

Round 2: Working continuously in the round, 2sc in each stitch (16 sts).

Round 3: Sc, 2sc in each stitch (24 sts), sl st to first stitch of round to join. Fasten off, leaving a long tail. With yarn needle, sew eyes into place.

Pupils (make 2)

Round 1: 4sc in first chain, sl st to first chain to create a ring.
Fasten off, leaving a long tail. Position pupils in desired location (looking to the side, up, down, cross-eyed, etc.) and sew into place with yarn needle.

Eyelashes (optional)

Using Color E, thread through yarn needle and weave in and out of bib to create eyelashes above eyes.

Ties

Using Color B, ch40, sc in each stitch across top of bib with right side facing you, ch41.
Turn, sc in first chain from hook and across (40), sl st 12 across top of bib, sc 40.
Fasten off. Weave in ends.

Teeth (make 2)

Using Color D, ch4.
Row 1: Turn, sc in first chain and across (3 sts).
Rows 2–8: Turn, ch1, sc in each stitch (3 sts).
Fasten off, leaving a long tail. Fold each tooth in half lengthwise and sew the 3 open sides together with yarn needle. Sew onto the bottom of the bib. Weave in ends.

Dress up your cutie's dress or sleeveless shirt with this fantastic shrug. This small wonder is great for spring, summer, or fall.

Finished Measurements

6–12 months: Shoulder to shoulder, 16.5"

Yarn
- Baby Bee Sweet Delight Baby, light worsted weight #3 yarn, 60% acrylic/40% polyamide (377 yd/4 oz per skein)
  - 1 skein #33 Little Princess

Hook and Other Materials

• F-3.75mm hook or size needed to obtain gauge **Gauge**
12 sts and 7 rows in dc = 3" square

Notes

1. The body is made in a single panel, sewn together, and then the trimming details are added.
2. The ch3 counts as the first stitch of each row.
3. For the Sleeve Trim and Inside Trim, the ch1 and ch2 do not count as stitches.
4. See page 112 for a tutorial on Double Crochet Decrease (dc dec).

Special Tech

Cluster

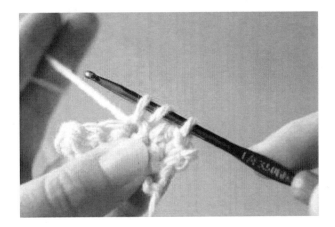

1. Yarn over, push hook through stitch, yarn over, and pull yarn back through: 3 loops on hook.

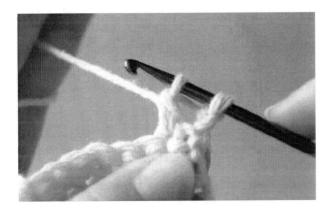

2. Yarn over, pull yarn through first 2 loops: 2 loops on hook.

3. Yarn over, push hook through SAME stitch, yarn over, and pull yarn back through: 4 loops on hook.

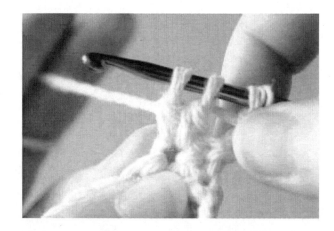

4. Yarn over, pull yarn through the first 2 loops: 3 loops on hook.

5. Yarn over, pull through all stitches. Cluster is complete.

Body

Ch47.

Row 1: Turn, dc in fourth chain from hook and in each across (44 sts).

Row 2: Turn, ch3, skip 1 stitch, *(cluster [see Special Technique], ch1, cluster) in next stitch, skip 2 stitches, repeat from * to last stitch. Dc in last stitch to complete row (44 sts).

Row 3: Turn, ch3, in each ch1 space (cluster, ch1, cluster) across. Dc in last stitch to complete row (44 sts).

Rows 4–28: Repeat Row 3.

Panel should measure 10" x 13".

Row 29: Turn, ch3, dc in each stitch (44 sts).

Fasten off.

Fold panel in half (panel will measure 5" x 13" folded). Using yarn needle, starting at one of the corners of the long edge, sew the 2 long edges together for 1.5". Cut and weave in ends. Repeat at the other corner of the long edge.

Sleeve Trim

Turn sewn panel right side out.

Round 1: Join yarn to outside edge of one of the seams, ch2, dc in same stitch, dc, dc dec (see Notes), *dc2, dc dec, repeat from* to complete round. End on dc2, sl st to first dc stitch of round to join.

Round 2: Ch2, dc in same stitch, dc, dc dec, *dc, dc dec, repeat from* to last stitch. Dc to finish round and sl st to first stitch of round to join (22 sts).

Rounds 3–4: Ch1, sc in each stitch, sl st to ch1 to join round (22 sts).

Round 5: Ch1, sl st to SAME stitch, *sl st to next stitch, ch3, sl st to SAME stitch, repeat from* to last stitch.

To finish, sl st to first stitch to join.

Fasten off.

Repeat for other sleeve. Weave in ends.

Inside Trim

Join yarn at right inside seam.

Round 1: Ch2, using ends of rows as stitches, 2dc in each, sl st to first stitch to join.

Rounds 2–3: Ch2, dc in same stitch and each stitch around, sl st to first stitch to join.

Rounds 4–5: Ch1, sc in each stitch to complete round, sl st to ch1 to join.

Round 6: Ch3, sl st to SAME stitch, *sl st to next stitch, ch3, sl st to SAME stitch, repeat from* to complete round, sl st to first stitch of round to join.

Fasten off. Weave in ends.

Every little boy needs a moose hat. Add a bow at the base of the antler and it's perfect for that special little girl, too.

Finished Measurements
Newborn: Circumference, 12–14"; Hat height, 5.5–6"
3–6 months: Circumference, 14–17"; Hat height, 6.5–7"
9–12 months: Circumference, 16–19"; Hat height, 7.5"

Yarn

- Red Heart Super Saver, medium worsted weight #4 yarn, 100% acrylic (364 yd/7 oz per skein)
    - 1 skein #0365 Dark Brown (Color A)
    - 1 skein #0336 Warm Brown (Color B)
    - 1 skein #0313 Aran (Color C)

Hook and Other Materials

- H-5.0mm hook or size needed to obtain gauge
- Stitch marker (optional)
- Yarn needle
- 2 medium black buttons
- Sewing thread and needle
- 2 pipe cleaners

Gauge

10 sts and 14 rows in sc = 3" square

Notes

1. The hat will be made first; the nose, eyes, and antlers will be added separately.
2. The hat is worked from the top down continuously in the round. If you like, mark the first stitch of the round with a stitch marker for reference.
3. Thread a pipe cleaner through each antler to help them hold their shape.
4. See page 109 for a tutorial on Single Crochet Decrease (sc dec) and page 115 on Treble Crochet (tr).

Special Technique

Special Technique

Cluster

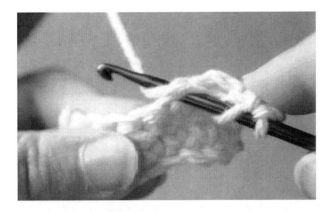

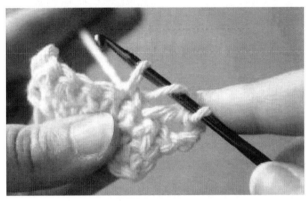

1. Yarn over, push hook through stitch, yarn over, and pull yarn back through: 3 loops on hook.

2. Yarn over, pull yarn through first 2 loops: 2 loops on hook.

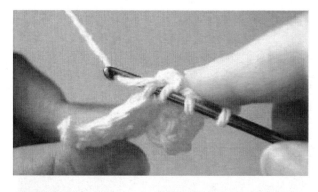

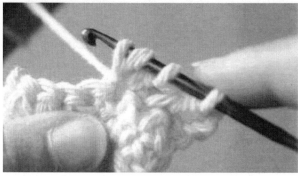

3. Yarn over, push hook through SAME stitch, yarn over, and pull yarn back through: 4 loops on hook.

4. Yarn over, pull yarn through first 2 loops: 3 loops on hook.

5. Yarn over, pull yarn through all loops. Cluster is complete.

Hat

Newborn

Using Color A, ch4, sl st to first chain to create a ring.

Round 1: Ch3 (this counts as your first dc), 9dc in ring (10 sts).

Round 2: Working continuously in the round, 2cluster (see Special Technique on pages 51–52) in each stitch (20 sts).

Round 3: *Cluster in first stitch, 2cluster in next stitch, repeat from to complete round (30 sts).*

Round 4: *Cluster3, 2cluster in next stitch, repeat from to complete round (40 sts).*

Rounds 5–9: Cluster in each stitch (40 sts).

Round 10: Sc in each stitch (40 sts).

Fasten off Color A. Join Color B.

Round 11: Sc in each stitch (40 sts).

Fasten off. Weave in ends.

3–6 Months

Using Color A, ch4, sl st to first chain to create a ring.

Round 1: Ch3 (this counts as your first dc), 9dc in ring (10 sts).

Round 2: Working continuously in the round, 2cluster (see Special Technique on pages 51–52) in each stitch (20 sts).

Round 3: *Cluster in first stitch, 2cluster in next stitch, repeat from to complete round (30 sts).*

Round 4: *Cluster3, 2cluster in next stitch, repeat from to complete round (40 sts).*

Round 5: *Cluster4, 2cluster in next stitch, repeat from to complete round (50* sts).

Rounds 6–12: Cluster in each stitch (50 sts).

Round 13: Sc in each stitch (50 sts).|

Fasten off Color A. Join Color B.

Round 14: Sc in each stitch (50 sts).

Fasten off. Weave in ends.

9–12 Months

Using Color A, ch4, sl st to first chain to create a ring.

Round 1: Ch3 (this counts as your first dc), 9dc in ring (10 sts).

Round 2: Working continuously in the round, 2cluster (see Special Technique on pages 51–52) in each stitch (20 sts).

Round 3: *Cluster, 2cluster in next stitch, repeat from* to complete round (30 sts).

Round 4: *Cluster3, 2cluster in next stitch, repeat from* to complete round (40 sts).

Round 5: *Cluster4, 2cluster in next stitch, repeat from* to complete round (50 sts).

Round 6: *Cluster5, 2cluster in next stitch, repeat from* to complete round (60 sts).

Rounds 7–14: Cluster in each stitch (60 sts).

Round 15: Sc in each stitch (60 sts).

Fasten off Color A. Join Color B.

Round 16: Sc in each stitch (60 sts).

Fasten off. Weave in ends.

Nose

Fold hat in half; mark each side of hat evenly with a stitch marker.

Newborn

Row 1: Join Color B at stitch marker, ch1, sc20 (20 sts).
Rows 2–10: Turn, sc20 (20 sts).
Row 11: Turn, sc dec (see [Notes](#)), sc16, sc dec (18 sts).
Row 12: Turn, sc dec, sc14, sc dec (16 sts).
Row 13: Turn, sc dec, sc12, sc dec (14 sts).
Row 14: Turn, sc dec, sc10, sc dec (12 sts).
Fasten off.

3–6 Months

Row 1: Join Color B at stitch marker, ch1, sc25 (25 sts).
Rows 2–10: Turn, sc25 (25 sts).
Row 11: Turn, sc dec (see [Notes](#)), sc21, sc dec (23 sts).
Row 12: Turn, sc dec, sc19, sc dec (21 sts).
Row 13: Turn, sc dec, sc17, sc dec (19 sts).
Row 14: Turn, sc dec, sc15, sc dec (17 sts).
Fasten off.

9–12 Months

Row 1: Join Color B at stitch marker, ch1, sc30 (30 sts).
Rows 2–10: Turn, sc30 (30 sts).
Row 11: Turn, sc dec (see [Notes](#)), sc26, sc dec (28 sts).
Row 12: Turn, sc dec, sc24, sc dec (26 sts).
Row 13: Turn, sc dec, sc22, sc dec (24 sts).
Row 14: Turn, sc dec, sc20, sc dec (22 sts).
Fasten off.

After completing the "nose," it will look like a flap on the edge of the beanie.

Join yarn at base of hat on bottom right of nose, ch1, sc around nose using ends of rows as stitches (see photo above). Fasten off, leaving a long tail. Using yarn needle, sew nose onto hat. Fasten off. Weave in ends.

Trim the nose with sc, using the ends of the rows as stitches.

Eyes (make 2)

Using Color C, ch5.

Round 1 Turn, sc3, 4sc in last stitch, working on opposite side of chain in the round sc3, 4sc in next stitch, sl st to first stitch to join (14sts).

Round 2: Ch1, sc4, 2sc in next stitch, sc, 2sc in next stitch, sc4, 2sc in next stitch, sc, 2sc in next stitch, sl st to ch1 to join (18 sts).

Fasten off, leaving a long tail.

Left Antler

Using 2 strands of Color B, ch15.

Row 1: 5dc in fifth chain from hook, ch1, sl st in same chain, skip 3 chains, (dc2, tr3 [see Notes], dc2, ch1, and sl st in same stitch) in next chain, skip 2 chains, dc2, (dc3, tr3, dc3) in last chain. Working on opposite side of chain row, dc, sc9 (to end).

Fasten off, leaving a long tail to sew onto the hat.

Right Antler

Using 2 strands of Color B, ch15.

Row 1: In fifth chain from hook (dc2, tr3, dc3), dc2, skip 2 chains, (2dc, 3tr, 3dc, ch1, and sl st to same stitch) in next chain, skip 3 chains, 5dc in next stitch, ch1, sl st to same chain, 3sc in last stitch. Working on opposite side of chain row, sc9, dc, sl st to third chain of first ch15. Fasten off, leaving a long tail to sew onto hat.

Finishing

Using yarn needle, attach the eyes, sewing around the last round.

Attach the antlers on either side 3 rows down from the top of the hat. Thread pipe cleaners through antlers (optional).

Weave in all ends.

Sew the buttons onto the white eyes with sewing needle and thread to finish.

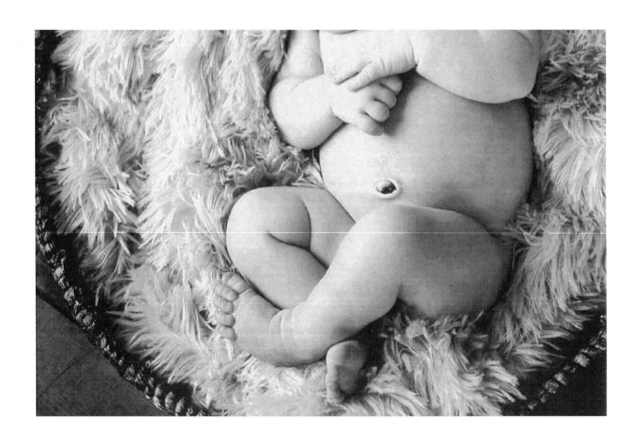

This sweet hat is a fun twist on the traditional beanie. The little knot topped off with a flower will surely bring a smile to any new mom!

Finished Measurements
Newborn: Circumference, 12–14"; Hat height, 5.5–6"

Yarn

- Peaches & Crème, medium worsted weight #4 yarn, 100% cotton (120 yd/2.5 oz per skein)

  1 skein #1740 Bright Pink (Color A)

  1 skein #1712 Bright Lime (Color B)

  1 skein #1612 Sunshine (Color C)

Hook and Other Materials

• H-5.0mm hook or size needed to obtain gauge • Stitch marker (optional)

Gauge
10 sts and 14 rows in sc = 3" square

Notes

1. You can make the hat in 1 solid color, with various stripes, or as directed.
2. The hat is worked from the top down continuously in the round. If you like, mark the first stitch of the round with a stitch marker for reference.
3. The flower is added at the end.
4. To change colors, push hook through the next stitch, pull yarn back through, yarn over with the NEXT color, and pull through. Color change is complete. See page 116 for a photo tutorial on changing colors.

Hat

Using Color A, ch4, sl st to first chain to create a ring.
Round 1: Ch1, sc in each chain (4 sts).
Rounds 2–25: Working continuously in the round, sc in each stitch (4 sts).
Round 26: 2sc in each stitch (8 sts).
Round 27: *Sc, 2sc in next stitch, repeat from* to complete round (12 sts).
Round 28: *Sc, 2sc in next stitch, repeat from* to complete round (18 sts).
Round 29: *Sc2, 2sc in next stitch, repeat from* to complete round (24 sts).
Round 30: *Sc3, 2sc in next stitch, repeat from* to complete round (30 sts).
Round 31: *Sc4, 2sc in next stitch, repeat from* to complete round (36 sts).
Rounds 32–45: Sc in each stitch (36 sts).
Fasten off Color A. Join Color B.
Round 46: Sc in each stitch (36 sts).

Fasten off Color B. Join Color C.

Round 47: Sc in each stitch, sl st to first stitch of round to join (36 sts).

Fasten off. Weave in ends.

Flower

Join Color B at end of tube on top of the hat.

Round 1: Ch1, sc in each chain, sl st to first ch1 to join (6 sts).

Round 2: In first stitch, (ch1, 2dc, ch1) and sl st to same stitch, *sl st to next stitch, (ch1, 2dc, ch1) in stitch, and sl st to same stitch, repeat from* to complete the petals (6 petals). Sl st to first ch1 of first petal to join.

Fasten off. Weave in ends to back of flower.

Using posts of the sc from Round 1, join Color B, loosely sl st around, and sl st to first slip stitch to join.

Fasten off. Weave in ends to back of flower.

Knot the tube loosely to finish.

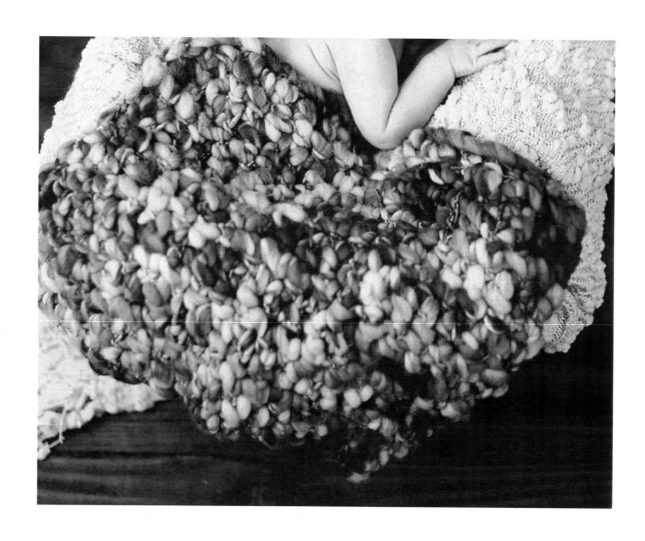

Keep your baby warm in the car with this sweet hat and blanket. The blanket is made with the softest yarn and is the perfect size to use in a car seat. The hat is adorable, with its fun pom on top.

Finished Measurements
Hat: Circumference, 12"; Hat height, 7" (excluding pom) Blanket: 12" x 16"

Yarn

- Heartstrings by Dee, Thick and Thin (*HeartstringsbyDee.etsy.com*), super bulky #6 yarn, 100% merino (90 yd/5.2 oz per skein)
    - 1 skein Teal and Brown Colorway (Color A)
- I Love This Cotton!, medium worsted weight #4 yarn, 100% cotton (180 yd/3.5 oz per skein)
    - 1 skein #24 Ivory (Color B)

Hooks and Other Materials
- Q-15.0mm hook or size needed to obtain gauge
- N-9.0mm hook or size needed to obtain gauge
- H-5.0mm hook or size needed to obtain gauge
- Stitch marker (optional)

Gauge

Hat: Using Color A and N-9.0mm hook, 7 sts and 9 rows in sc = 3" square Hat: Using Color B and H-5.0 hook, 11 sts and 6 rows in dc = 3" square Blanket: Using Color A and Q-15.0mm hook, 4 sts and 3 rows in sc = 3" square **Hat Notes**

1. The hat pattern is worked from the bottom up.
2. The slip stitches in Rounds 2–5 need to be worked loosely. Do not pull tight. The Color A yarn is naturally bulky and thin in different sections. If you work tightly, the texture will be diminished.
3. Count the first ch1 as a stitch in the first 3 rounds. When joining each round, sl st to first ch1 stitch.
4. After joining Color B, you will work continuously in the round until the hat is complete. If you like, mark the first stitch of the round with a stitch marker for reference.
5. See page 120 for a tutorial on how to make a pom and page 107 for working the back loop only (blo) of a stitch.
6. The hat is made to be a little slouchy, with the pom resting on top.

Blanket Notes
1. You will use the Q-15.0mm afghan hook for this mini blanket.
2. Work loosely. The Color A yarn is naturally bulky and thin in different sections. If you work tightly, the texture will be diminished.
3. See page 110 for a tutorial on Half Double Crochet (hdc).

Hat

Using Color A and N-9.0mm hook, ch33, sl st to first chain to create a ring.
Round 1: Ch1, sc in first chain and around, sl st in first ch1 to join (32 sts).
Round 2: Ch1, loosely sl st in each stitch, sl st in first ch1 to join (32 sts).
Round 3: Ch1, sl st in each stitch in blo (see Notes), sl st in first ch1 to join (32 sts).
Rounds 4–5: Repeat Round 3.
Fasten off Color A, join Color B. Use H-5.0mm hook to complete hat.
Round 6: Ch3, dc in each stitch in blo, do not sl st to join.
Rounds 7–18: Working in the round, dc in each stitch through both loops. To finish, hdc in next stitch, sc in next stitch, sl st to next stitch.
Fasten off, leaving a long tail to weave the top together.
With H-5.0 hook, weave the tail in and out of every other stitch to gather the top. Pull the yarn tightly to cinch the top. Secure the ends.

Pom

Make a pom with Color A (see Notes) and attach to the top.

Blanket

Using Color A and Q-15.0mm hook, ch22.
Row 1: Loosely sc in second chain from hook and in each stitch across (21 sts).
Row 2: Turn, ch3, hdc (see Notes) in next stitch, dc in next stitch, *hdc, dc, repeat from* to complete row.
Row 3: Turn, ch1, sc in each stitch.
Rows 4 to end: Repeat Rows 2 and 3 to complete, using up the remaining skein of Color A.
Fasten off. Weave in ends.

Baby Pants

These pants are not only cute, but they're also easy to make! The Denimstyle yarn by Bernat is super soft and cozy and is the best alternative to scratchy jeans.

Finished Measurements

3–6 months: Waist, 7"; Length, 12"
6–9 months: Waist, 8"; Length, 14"
9–12 months: Waist, 9"; Length, 16"

Yarn

- Bernat Denimstyle, medium worsted weight #4 yarn, 70% acrylic/30% cotton (196 yd/3.5 oz per skein) 1 skein #03044 Sweatshirt (Color A)
- I Love This Yarn!, medium worsted weight #4 yarn, 100% acrylic (251 yd/5 oz per skein) 1 skein #3950 Charcoal (Color B)

Hook and Other Materials
- G-4.50mm hook or size needed to obtain gauge
- Stitch markers

Gauge

10 sts and 9 rows in hdc = 3" square

Notes

1. The pants are worked from the top down continuously in the round. If you like, mark the first stitch of the round with a stitch marker for reference.
2. See page 110 for a tutorial on Half Double Crochet (hdc).
3. The pocket and carpenter strap are made separately and sewn on.

Pants

3–6 Months

Using Color A, ch40, sl st to first chain to create a ring (40 ch).

Round 1: Ch2, hdc (see Notes) in each chain, do not join (40 sts).

Rounds 2–10: Working continuously in the round, hdc in each stitch (40 sts).

Round 11: Hdc10, place a stitch marker on stitch 20, hdc20, place a stitch marker on stitch 30, hdc to complete round (40 sts).

Leg 1

Round 12: Hdc10 to first stitch marker, hdc in same stitch as second stitch marker, hdc to complete round (20 sts). First round of Leg 1 is complete.

Rounds 13–26: Working continuously in the round, hdc in each stitch (20 sts).

Fasten off Color A, join Color B.

Rounds 27–31: Hdc in each stitch (20 sts). To finish, sl st to first stitch of round.

Fasten off. Weave in ends.

Leg 2

Join Color A in center of pants on Round 11.

Round 12: Ch2, hdc in same stitch as the ch2, hdc in each stitch to complete round (20 sts).

Rounds 13–26: Working continuously in the round, hdc in each stitch (20 sts).

Fasten off Color A, join Color B.

Rounds 27–31: Hdc in each stitch (20 sts). To finish, sl st to first stitch of round.

Fasten off. Weave in ends.

6–9 Months

Using Color A, ch60, sl st to first chain to create a ring (60 ch).

Round 1: Ch2, hdc (see Notes) in each chain, do not join (60 sts).

Rounds 2–13: Working continuously in the round, hdc in each stitch (60 sts).

Round 14: Hdc15, place a stitch marker on stitch 15, hdc30, place a stitch marker on stitch 45, hdc to end of round (60 sts).

Leg 1

Round 15: Hdc15 to first stitch marker, hdc in same stitch as second stitch marker, hdc to complete round (30 sts).

First round of Leg 1 is complete.

Rounds 16–31: Working continuously in the round, hdc in each stitch (30 sts).

Fasten off Color A, join Color B.

Rounds 32–36: Hdc in each stitch (30 sts). To finish, sl st to first stitch of round. Fasten off. Weave in ends.

Leg 2

Join Color A in center of pants on Round 14.

Round 15: Ch2, hdc in same stitch as the ch2, hdc in each stitch to complete round (30 sts).

Rounds 16–31: Working continuously in the round, hdc in each stitch (30 sts).

Fasten off Color A, join Color B.

Rounds 32–36: Hdc in each stitch (30 sts). To finish, sl st to first stitch of round. Fasten off. Weave in ends.

9–12 Months

Using Color A, ch70, sl st to first chain to create a ring (80 ch).

Round 1: Ch2, hdc (see Notes) in each chain, do not join (80 sts).

Rounds 2–15: Working continuously in the round, hdc in each stitch (80 sts).

Round 16: Hdc20, place a stitch marker on stitch 20, hdc40, place a stitch marker on stitch 60, hdc to end of round (80 sts).

Leg 1

Round 17: Hdc20 to first stitch marker, hdc in same stitch as second stitch marker, hdc to end of round (40 sts). First round of Leg 1 is complete.

Rounds 18–34: Working continuously in the round, hdc in each stitch (40 sts).

Fasten off Color A, join Color B.

Rounds 35–39: Hdc in each stitch (40 sts). To finish, sl st to first stitch of round. Fasten off. Weave in ends.

Leg 2

Join Color A in center of pants on Round 16.

Round 17: Ch2, hdc in same stitch as the ch2, hdc in each stitch to complete

round (40 sts).
Rounds 18–34: Working continuously in the round, hdc in each stitch (40 sts). Fasten off Color A, join Color B.
Rounds 35–39: Hdc in each stitch (40 sts). To finish, sl st to first stitch of round. Fasten off. Weave in ends.

Waistband Trim

Join Color B in back center at waist.
Round 1: Ch2, dc in the same stitch as the ch2, dc in each stitch to complete round, sl st to first dc (not ch2) to join (60 sts).
Round 2: Repeat Round 1.
Round 3: Ch1, sc in each stitch to complete round, sl st to ch1 to join (60 sts).
Fasten off. Weave in ends.

Drawstring

Using Color A, ch90. Fasten off. Weave in ends.
Starting at front middle of waistband trim, thread drawstring in and out of Round 2. Tie loosely.

Pocket

Using Color B, ch13.
Row 1: Turn, sc in first chain and across (12 sts).
Rows 2–12: Turn, sc in first stitch and across (12 sts).
Fasten off, leaving a long tail to sew onto the pants.
Leaving the top open, sew the 3 sides of the pocket onto the side of Leg 1. Weave in ends.

Carpenter's Strap

Using Color B, ch13.
Row 1: Turn, sc in first chain and across (12 sts).
Rows 2–4: Turn, sc in each stitch (12 sts).
Fasten off.
Sew the 2 ends onto the pants, leaving the top and bottom open.

The open-weave beanie's open design is perfect for a year-round accessory. Use it in the spring, summer, and fall as light accessory, or dress it up for the holidays and winter for a sweet beanie. Coordinate to match any outfit!.

Finished Measurements

Newborn: Circumference, 12–14";
    Hat height, 5.5–6"
3–6 months: Circumference, 14–17";
    Hat height, 6.5–7"
9–12 months: Circumference, 16–19"; Hat height, 7.5"

Yarn

- Yarn Bee I Love This Cotton!, medium worsted weight #4 yarn, 100% cotton (180 yd/3.5 oz per skein)

    1 skein #24 Ivory (Color A)
    1 skein #254 Rosy (Color B)
    1 skein #48 Taupe (Color C)
    1 skein #40 Sage (Color D)

Hook and Other Materials

• F-3.75mm hook or size needed to obtain gauge

• Stitch marker (optional)

• Yarn needle

Gauge

18 sts and 15 rows in sc = 3" square

Notes

1. The hat will be made first and flowers added last.
2. The hat is worked from the top down continuously in the round. If you like, mark the first stitch of the round with a stitch marker for reference.
3. See page 109 for a tutorial on Single Crochet Decrease (sc dec) and page 115 for Treble Crochet (tr).

Beanie

Newborn

Using Color A, ch4, sl st to first chain to create a ring.

Round 1: Ch1 (this counts as your first sc), 7sc in ring (8 sts).

Round 2: Working continuously in the round, 2sc in each stitch (16 sts).

Round 3: *Sc, 2sc in next stitch, repeat from* to complete round (24 sts).

Round 4: *Sc2, 2sc in next stitch, repeat from* to complete round (32 sts).

Round 5: *Skip 2 stitches, ch1, 3dc in next stitch, repeat from* to complete round (44 sts).

Round 6: (3dc, ch1) in each ch1 space to complete round.

Rounds 7–10: Repeat Round 6.

Rounds 11–16: Fasten off Color A, join Color C. Sc in each stitch. To finish, sl st to first stitch of round (44 sts).

Fasten off and weave in ends.

3–6 Months

Using Color A, ch4, sl st to first chain to create a ring.

Round 1: Ch1 (this counts as your first sc), 7sc in ring (8 sts).

Round 2: Working continuously in the round, 2sc in each stitch (16 sts).

Round 3: *Sc, 2sc in next stitch, repeat from* to complete round (24 sts).

Round 4: *Sc2, 2sc in next stitch, repeat from* to complete round (32 sts).

Round 5: *Sc3, 2sc in next stitch, repeat from* to complete round (40 sts).

Round 6: *Skip 2 stitches, ch1, 3dc in next stitch, repeat from* to complete round (52 sts).

Round 7: (3dc, ch1) in each ch1 space to complete round (52 sts).

Rounds 8–13: Repeat Round 7.

Round 14: Fasten off Color A, join Color C. Sc in each stitch (52 sts).

Rounds 15–20: Working continuously in the round, sc in each stitch (52 sts). To finish, sl st to first stitch of round.

Fasten off. Weave in ends.

9–12 Months

Using Color A, ch4, sl st to first chain to create a ring.

Round 1: Ch1 (this counts as your first sc), 7sc in ring (8 sts).

Round 2: Working continuously in the round, 2sc in each stitch (16 sts).

Round 3: *Sc, 2sc in next stitch, repeat from* to complete round (24 sts).

Round 4: *Sc2, 2sc in next stitch, repeat from* to complete round (32 sts).

Round 5: *Sc3, 2sc in next stitch, repeat from* to complete round (40 sts).

Round 6: *Sc4, 2sc in next stitch, repeat from* to complete round (48 sts).

Round 7: *Skip 2 stitches, ch1, 3dc in next stitch, repeat from* to complete round (60 sts).

Round 8: (3dc, ch1) in each ch1 space to complete round (60 sts).

Rounds 9–16: Repeat Round 8.

Round 17: Fasten off Color A, join Color C. Sc in each stitch (60 sts).

Rounds 18–23: Working continuously in the round, sc in each stitch (60 sts). To finish, sl st to next first stitch of round.

Fasten off. Weave in ends.

Flower Stack

First Flower (bottom)

Using Color B, ch5, sl st to first chain to create a ring.

Round 1: Ch1, 8sc in ring, sl st to first sc to join (8 sts).

Round 2: (Ch1, 2dc, tr [see Notes], 2dc, ch1) in next stitch, sl st to same stitch, *sl st to next stitch, (ch1, 2dc, tr, 2dc, ch1) in next stitch, sl st to same stitch, repeat from* to complete petals, sl st to first ch1 to join round (8 petals).

Fasten off. Weave in ends.

Second Flower

Using Color A, ch5, sl st to first chain to create a ring.

Round 1: Ch1, 6sc in ring, sl st to first sc to join (6 sts).

Round 2: (Ch1, 2dc, tr, 2dc, ch1) in next stitch, sl st to same stitch, *sl st to next stitch, (ch1, 2dc, tr, 2dc, ch1) sl st to same stitch, repeat from* to complete round, sl st to first ch1 to join (6 petals). Fasten off. Weave in ends.

Third Flower

Using Color B, ch4, sl st to first chain to create a ring.

Round 1: Ch1, 6sc in ring, sl st to first sc to join (6 sts).

Round 2: Ch1, 3dc in same stitch, ch1, sl st to same stitch, *sl st to next stitch, ch1, 3dc in same stitch, ch1, sl st to same stitch, repeat from* to complete round, sl st to first ch1 to join (6 petals).

Fasten off. Weave in ends.

Fourth Flower

Using Color A, ch4, sl st to first chain to create a ring.

Round 1: Ch1, 5sc in ring, sl st to first sc to join (5 sts).

Round 2: Ch1, 2dc in same stitch, ch1, sl st to same stitch, *sl st to next stitch, ch1, 2dc in same stitch, ch1, sl st to same stitch, repeat from* to complete round, sl st to first ch1 to join (5 petals).

Fasten off. Weave in ends.

Leaves (make 2)

Using Color D, ch6.

Row 1: Turn, sc in first chain from hook and across (5 sts).

Rows 2–6: Turn, ch1, sc across (5 sts).

Row 7: Turn, sc dec (see Notes), sc, sc dec (3 sts).
Row 8: Turn, sc dec, use middle stitch again and sc dec (2 sts).
Row 9: Turn, sc dec, sl st to finish (1 st).
Fasten off. Weave in ends.

Finishing

Stack the flowers together with the first flower in back to the fifth flower on top. Use Color B and yarn needle to sew flowers together through the middle rings. Sew leaves to base of back flower. After flowers are sewn together and leaves are added, sew onto hat securely.

Puppy Hat

"How cute is that puppy!" Yes, that's exactly what your friends and family will be saying every time they see your baby in this hat.

Finished Measurements

Newborn: Circumference, 12–14"; Hat height, 5.5–6"
3–6 months: Circumference, 14–17"; Hat height, 6.5–7"
9–12 months: Circumference, 16–19"; Hat height, 7.5"

Yarn

- Lion Brand Jiffy, bulky weight #5 yarn, 100% acrylic (135 yd/3 oz per skein)
    1 skein #450-126 Espresso (Color A)
    1 skein #450-098 Oat (Color B)

Hook and Other Materials
• H-5.0mm hook or size needed to obtain gauge
• Yarn needle
• 2 small black buttons (for the eyes)
• 1 large black button (for the nose)
• Sewing thread and needle

Gauge

9 sts and 12 rows in hdc = 3" square

Notes

1. You will make the hat and all the parts first. The ears, eyes, and spots will be added last using a yarn needle.
2. The hat is worked from the top down continuously in the round. If you like, mark the first stitch of the round with a stitch marker for reference.
3. See page 110 for a tutorial on Half Double Crochet (hdc) and page 109 for Single Crochet Decrease (sc dec).
4. The ears can be made longer or shorter by increasing or decreasing the length of Rows 8–33.

Hat

Newborn

Using Color A, ch4, sl st to first chain to create a ring.

Round 1: Ch2 (this counts as your first hdc), 7hdc (see Notes) in ring (8 sts).
Round 2: Working continuously in the round, 2hdc in each stitch (16 sts).
Round 3: *Hdc, 2hdc in next stitch, repeat from* to complete round (24 sts).
Round 4: *Hdc2, 2hdc in next stitch, repeat from* to complete round (32 sts).
Rounds 5–16: Hdc in each stitch, sl st to first stitch of round to join (32 sts).
Fasten off. Weave in ends.

3–6 Months

Using Color A, ch4, sl st to first chain to create a ring.

Round 1: Ch2 (this counts as your first hdc), 7hdc (see Notes) in ring (8 sts).
Round 2: Working continuously in the round, 2hdc in each stitch (16 sts).
Round 3: *Hdc, 2hdc in next stitch, repeat from* to complete round (24 sts).
Round 4: *Hdc2, 2hdc in next stitch, repeat from* to complete round (32 sts).
Round 5: *Hdc3, 2hdc in next stitch, repeat from* to complete round (40 sts).
Rounds 6–20: Hdc in each stitch, sl st to first stitch of round to join (40 sts).
Fasten off. Weave in ends.

9–12 Months

Using Color A, ch4, sl st to first chain to create a ring.

Round 1: Ch2 (this counts as your first hdc), 7hdc (see Notes) in ring (8 sts).
Round 2: Working continuously in the round, 2hdc in each stitch (16 sts).
Round 3: *Hdc, 2hdc in next stitch, repeat from* to complete round (24 sts).
Round 4: *Hdc2, 2hdc in next stitch, repeat from* to complete round (32 sts).

Round 5: *Hdc3, 2hdc in next stitch, repeat from* to complete round (40 sts).
Round 6: *Hdc4, 2hdc in next stitch, repeat from* to complete round (48 sts).
Rounds 7–24: Hdc in each stitch, sl st to first stitch of round to join (48 sts).
Fasten off. Weave in ends.

Eye Patch

Using Color B, ch4, sl st to first chain to create a ring.
Round 1: Ch1, 5sc in ring (6 sts).
Round 2: Working continuously in the round, 2sc in each stitch (12 sts).
Round 3: *Sc, 2sc in next stitch, repeat from* to complete round (18 sts).
Round 4: *Sc2, 2sc in next stitch, repeat from* to complete round (24 sts). Sl st to first stitch of round to join.
Fasten off, leaving a long tail to sew onto hat. Weave in other end.

Ear Spot

Using Color B, ch4, sl st to first chain to create a ring.
Round 1: Ch1, 5sc in ring (6 sts).
Round 2: 2sc in each stitch (12 sts). Sl st to first stitch of round to join.
Fasten off, leaving a long tail to sew onto ear. Weave in other end.

Ears (make 1 in each color)

Ch5.
Row 1: Turn, sc in first chain and across (4 sts).
Row 2: Turn, ch1, sc in first stitch and across (4 sts).
Rows 3–6: Repeat Row 2.
Row 7: Turn, ch1, sc in same stitch, sc across to next to last stitch, 2sc in last stitch (6 sts).
Rows 8–33: Turn, ch1, sc in first stitch and across (6 sts).
Row 34: Turn, sc dec (see Notes), sc2, sc dec (4 sts).
Fasten off. Weave in ends.

Ear Trim

With the front side of the ear facing you, join same color yarn at top left at first chain. Using ends of rows as stitches, ch1, sc around ear, sl st to ch1 to join. Fasten off, leaving a long tail to sew onto hat. Weave in other end. Repeat with the other ear.

Finishing

Sew each ear onto the hat 3 rows down from the top of the beanie. Sew the eye patch onto 1 side. Sew the ear spot onto 1 of the ears. To finish, using sewing needle and thread, sew the 2 buttons on for eyes and the 1 button on for the nose. Weave in ends.

I have always thought of ponchos as being old-fashioned and not stylish at all, but this yarn inspired me to rethink the poncho in a fresh new way. Have fun with the color and add a shell edge for a pretty detail to make this poncho perfect for your favorite girly girl!

Finished Measurements

6–12 months: Shoulder to shoulder,
14" (trim included); Length:
10" (collar included)
(For other sizes, see Notes.)

Yarn

- Yarn Bee Danielle, medium worsted weight #4 yarn, 90% acrylic/10% polyamide (207 yd/3.5 oz)

     2 skeins #62 Rosalinda

Hook and Other Materials
- H-5.0mm hook or size needed to obtain gauge
- Yarn needle
- Medium button (optional)
- Sewing thread and needle (optional)

Gauge

14 sts and 7 rows in dc = 3" square

Notes

1. The poncho is worked out from the top center in rows in 2 panels.
2. The first ch3 of each row is counted as a double crochet stitch for the current row.
3. See page 107 for a tutorial on working in the front loop only (flo) or the back loop only (blo) of a stitch. Doing this will create a textured pattern throughout the poncho.
4. To increase size of finished poncho: At Row 9, continue repeating Rows 7 and 8 until the desired length is reached. Each row will increase by 6 stitches.
5. To decrease size of finished poncho: Either follow the pattern as is using a smaller hook or, at Row 9, repeat Rows 7 and 8 fewer times.
6. The collar is optional and can be made with a simple single crochet trim instead if preferred.
7. The flower is optional.

Poncho (make 2 panels)

Ch4.

Row 1: (2dc, ch2, 3dc) in first chain (8 sts).

Row 2: Turn, ch3 (counts as a dc here and throughout), dc in same stitch, dc2, (2dc, ch2, 2dc) in ch2 space, dc2, 2dc in last stitch (14 sts).

Row 3: Turn, ch3, dc in same stitch in flo (see Notes), dc5, (2dc, ch2, 2dc) in ch2 space, dc5, 2dc in last stitch (20 sts).

Row 4: Turn, ch3, dc in same stitch in blo (see Notes), dc8, (2dc, ch2, 2dc) in ch2 space, dc8, 2dc in last stitch (26 sts).

Row 5: Turn, ch3, dc in flo of same stitch, dc11, (2dc, ch2, 2dc) in ch2 space, dc11, 2dc in last stitch (32 sts).

Row 6: Turn, ch3, dc in blo of same stitch, dc14, (2dc, ch2, 2dc) in ch2 space, dc14, 2dc in last stitch (38 sts).

Row 7: Turn, ch3, dc in flo of same stitch, dc to ch2 space, (2dc, ch2, 2dc) in ch2 space, dc to last stitch, 2dc in last stitch.

Row 8: Turn, ch3, dc in blo of same stitch, dc to ch2 space, (2dc, ch2, 2dc) in ch2 space, dc to last stitch, 2dc in last stitch.

Rows 9–16: Repeat Rows 7 and 8.

Fasten off.

Align the 2 panels together, right sides facing out, and use the yarn needle to sew 11 rows in from each side, leaving the center open.

Shell Edge

Join yarn on one of the seams on the outside corner of poncho, ch1, *skip 2 stitches, sl st in next stitch, skip 2 stitches, 5dc in next stitch, repeat from* to ch2 space in bottom corner, (2sc, ch2, 2sc) in ch2 space, skip 2 stitches, 5dc in next stitch, repeat from * to end, sl st to ch1 to join.

Collar (optional)

If an open-neck poncho is preferred, simply join the yarn and sc around the opening to trim.

Round 1: Join yarn at right side seam. Ch2, using ends of rows as stitches, 2sc in each stitch around sl st to first sc stitch to join.

Round 2: Ch2, dc in same stitch and each stitch to complete round, sl st to first dc stitch join.

Round 3: Repeat Round 2.

Round 4: Turn, ch2, working in blo throughout round dc in same stitch and in each stitch to complete round, sl st to first dc stitch to join.

Rounds 5–6: Ch2, dc in same stitch and in each stitch to complete round, sl st to first stitch to join.

Round 7: Ch1, loosely sl st in each stitch, sl st to ch1 to join.

Fasten off. Weave in ends.

Back Flower

Ch5, sl st to first chain to create a ring.

Round 1: Ch1, 8sc in ring, sl st to first sc stitch to join (8 sts).

Round 2: Ch1, dc, ch1, sl st to same stitch, *sl st to next stitch, ch1, dc, ch1, sl st to same stitch, repeat from * to complete round, sl st to first ch1 to join (8 petals).

The flowers will easily slip over the button.

Top Flower

Ch5, sl st to first chain to create a ring.

Round 1: Ch1, 6sc in ring, sl st to first sc stitch to join (6sts).

Round 2: Ch1, dc, ch1, sl st to same stitch, *sl st to next stitch, ch1, dc, ch1, sl st to same stitch, repeat from * to complete round, sl st to first ch1 to join (6 petals).

Finishing

Securely sew the button with sewing thread and needle onto the poncho wherever you prefer and slip the center of each flower over the button.

With its warmth and comfort, this is a wonderful blanket for any baby. It has a beautiful design with very lush edging on the ends, which gives great texture contrasts for your child to explore.

Finished Measurements

30" x 40"

Yarn

- Jo-Ann Sensations, bulky weight #5 yarn, 50% acrylic/50% polyamide (120 yd/3.5 oz)
     2 skeins #1316 Rosario Multi (Color A)
- Lion Brand Pound of Love, medium worsted weight #4 yarn, 100% acrylic (1,020 yd/16 oz)
     1 skein #550-099 Antique White (Color B)

Hook and Other Materials
- N-9.0mm hook or size needed to obtain gauge

Gauge
6 sts and 2 rows in dc = 3" square

Notes
1. Work loosely with Color A.
2. The ch1, ch2, or ch3 at the beginning of each row is the first stitch of that row. In return, it is the last stitch of the next row.
3. See page 110 for a tutorial on Half Double Crochet (hdc) and page 113 for Front Post Double Crochet (fpdc).
4. The length can be increased by repeating Rows 11–14 after Row 69. Continue with Row 70 to finish.

Blanket

Using Color A, ch77.

Row 1: Turn, dc in fourth chain from hook (73 sts).

Row 2: Turn, ch1, sc in next stitch, *skip 2 stitches, (sc, hdc, dc) in next stitch, repeat from* to third to last stitch, skip next stitch, sc in last stitch to complete row.

Row 3: Turn, ch3, dc in next stitch (the ch3 counts as first dc here and throughout) and across.

Row 4: Turn, ch1, sc in next stitch, *skip 2 stitches, (dc, hdc [see Notes], sc) in next stitch, repeat from * to third-tolast stitch, skip next stitch, sc in last stitch to complete row.

Row 5: Turn, ch1, sc in each stitch.

Row 6: Repeat Row 5.

Row 7: Turn, ch3, dc in next stitch and across.

Row 8: Repeat Row 2.

Row 9: Turn, ch3, dc in next stitch and across.

Row 10: Join Color B, turn, ch1, sc in next stitch and across.

Row 11: Turn, ch2, hdc in each stitch across.

Row 12: Turn, ch1, sc in next stitch and across.

Row 13: Turn, ch3, *dc in next stitch, fpdc (see Notes) on dc you just created, skip 1 stitch, repeat from * to next to last stitch, dc in last stitch to complete row.

Row 14: Turn, ch1, sc in next stitch and across.

Row 15–69: Repeat Rows 11–14.

Fasten off Color B.

Rows 70–78: Join Color A, repeat Rows 9, 8, 7, 6, 5, 4, 3, 2, 1 in that order to complete matching end to blanket.

Fasten off. Weave in ends.

This beanie not only is adorable, but it can also be personalized for a boy or girl. You'll be the hit of the baby shower. And being from Alabama, I'll be the first to say, "Roll Tide!"

Finished Measurements

Newborn: Circumference, 12–14"; Hat height, 5.5–6"
3–6 months: Circumference, 14–17"; Hat height, 6.5–7"
9–12 months: Circumference, 16–19"; Hat height, 7.5"

Yarn

- Red Heart Super Saver, medium worsted weight #4 yarn, 100% acrylic (364 yd/7 oz)

    1 skein #3950 Charcoal (Color A)
    1 skein #373 Petal Pink (Color B)

Hook and Other Materials
• H-5.0mm hook or size needed to obtain gauge
• Yarn needle
• Stitch markers

Gauge
10 sts and 9 rows in sc = 3" square

Notes

1. The beanie is worked from the top down continuously in the round. If you like, mark the first stitch of the round with a stitch marker for reference.
2. The beanie and ears are made separately and sewn together.
3. See page 110 for a tutorial on Half Double Crochet (hdc).

Special Technique

Cluster

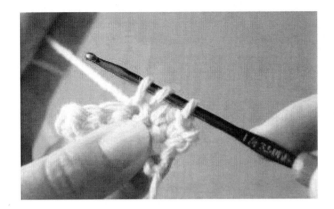

1. Yarn over, push hook through stitch, yarn over, and pull yarn back through: 3 loops on hook.

2. Yarn over, pull yarn through first 2 loops: 2 loops on hook.

3. Yarn over, push hook through SAME stitch, yarn over, and pull yarn back through: 4 loops on hook.

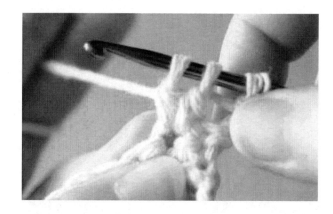

4. Yarn over, pull yarn through first 2 loops: 3 loops on hook.

5. Yarn over, pull yarn through all stitches. Cluster is complete.

Beanie

Newborn

Using Color A, ch4, sl st to first chain to create a ring.

Round 1: Ch1 (this counts as your first sc), 7sc in ring (8 sts).

Round 2: Working continuously in the round, 2hdc (see Notes) in each stitch (16 sts).

Round 3 *Sc, 2sc in next stitch, repeat from* to complete round (24 sts).

Round 4: *Hdc2, 2hdc in next stitch, repeat from* to complete round (32 sts).

Round 5: Sc in each stitch (32 sts).

Round 6: Hdc in each stitch (32 sts).

Rounds 7–16: Repeat Rounds 5 and 6. To finish, sl st to first stitch of round. Fasten off. Weave in ends.

3–6 Months

Using Color A, ch4, sl st to first chain to create a ring.

Round 1: Ch1 (this counts as your first sc), 7sc in ring (8 sts).

Round 2: Working continuously in the round, 2hdc (see Notes) in each stitch (16 sts).

Round 3: *Sc, 2sc in next stitch, repeat from* to complete round (24 sts).
Round 4: *Hdc2, 2hdc in next stitch, repeat from* to complete round (32 sts).
Round 5: *Sc3, 2sc in next stitch, repeat from* to complete round (40 sts).
Round 6: Hdc in each stitch (40 sts).
Round 7: Sc in each stitch (40 sts).
Rounds 8–20: Repeat Rounds 6 and 7. To finish, sl st to first stitch of round. Fasten off. Weave in ends.

9–12 Months

Using Color A, ch4, sl st to first chain to create a ring.
Round 1: Ch1 (this counts as your first sc), 7sc in ring (8 sts).
Round 2: Working continuously in the round, 2hdc (see Notes) in each stitch (16 sts).
Round 3: *Sc, 2sc in next stitch, repeat from* to complete round (24 sts).
Round 4: *Hdc2, 2hdc in next stitch, repeat from* to complete round (32 sts).
Round 5: *Sc3, 2sc in next stitch, repeat from* to complete round (40 sts).
Round 6: *Hdc4, 2hdc in next stitch, repeat from* to complete round (48 sts).
Round 7: Sc in each stitch (48 sts).
Round 8: Hdc in each stitch (48 sts).
Rounds 9–24: Repeat Rounds 7 and 8. To finish, sl st to first stitch of round. Fasten off. Weave in ends.

Ears

Make 2 of each section, 1 in each color. To make the ears for 3–6 months, repeat the last round for the top and bottom parts one time. To make the ears for 6–12 months, repeat the last round for the top and bottom parts twice.

Newborn

Top

Ch2.
Round 1: 6sc in first chain (6 sts).
Round 2: Working in the round, 2sc in each stitch (12 sts).
Round 3: *Sc, 2sc in next stitch, repeat from* to complete round (18 sts).
Round 4: *Sc2, 2sc in next stitch, repeat from* to complete round (24 sts).
Fasten off.

Bottom

Ch2.

Round 1: 6sc in first chain (6 sts).

Round 2: Working in the round, 2sc in each stitch (12 sts).

Round 3: *Sc, 2sc in next stitch, repeat from* to complete round (18 sts). Fasten off.

Using 4 stitches to join, sew the top and bottom sections of each color together with the yarn needle.

Next, sew the pink onto the gray, making it 1 piece.

Next, trim will be added to the outside of each ear.

Right Ear

Place 1 ear in front of you, pink side up, with the smaller side closest to you. Locate the center stitch at the bottom and count 4 stitches to the left. Place a stitch marker. Now, locate the center stitch at the top of the ear, count 6 stitches to the left, and place a marker.

At the marker on the bottom, join Color A, ch3, and cluster (see Special Technique on <u>page 73</u>) in each stitch around the outside of the ear. When you reach the center point where the circles join, sl st, then cluster in each stitch around the top section until you reach the second stitch marker. Fasten off.

Left Ear

Place the other ear in front of you, pink side up, with the smaller side closest to you. Locate the center stitch at the bottom and count 4 stitches to the right. Place a stitch marker. Now, locate the center stitch at the top of the ear, count 6 stitches to the right, and place a marker.

At the marker on the bottom, join Color A, ch3, and cluster (see <u>Special Technique</u>) in each stitch around the outside of the ear. When you reach the center point where the circles join, sl st, then cluster in each stitch around the top section until you reach the second stitch marker. Fasten off.

Sew the ears onto the hat with the yarn needle. Weave in ends.

Hair Sprigs

Cut 8 to 10 lengths of Color A approximately 4" long. Fold the lengths in half, pull the folded center of the lengths through the first ch4 ring, and finish by pulling the ends through the loop (like fringe). Trim evenly.

1. Push hook through first round of hat, and pull center of yarn strands through.

2. Pull ends of strands through loop and pull tight. Repeat around ring.

3. Trim evenly.

This classy sweater is perfect for any occasion: preppy or play. Dress it up or down for boys or girls, and you'll have the most stylish baby on the block.

Finished Measurements

6–12 months: Chest when buttoned, 20"; Sweater length,
   11.5"; Sleeve length (from bottom of row where the sleeve begins to end),
8.5"
(For other sizes, see Notes.)

Yarn

- Yarn Bee I Love This Yarn!, medium worsted weight #4 yarn, 100% acrylic (355 yd/7 oz per skein)
    1 skein #839324 Ivory (Color A)
- Lion Brand Vanna's Choice, medium worsted weight #4 yarn, 100% acrylic (170 yd/4 oz)
    1 skein #860-108 Dusty Blue (Color B)

Hook and Other Materials

• G-4.50mm hook or size needed to obtain gauge
• 5 medium buttons in chocolate brown
• Sewing needle and thread

Gauge
9 sts and 5 rows in dc = 2" square

Notes

1. Pattern is worked in rows for the main body, in the round for the sleeves.
2. Working the body of the sweater, the first ch3 is counted as a dc stitch.
3. The sleeves are worked out of the armholes of the sweater.
4. The edging is added after the main body is completed.
5. When slip stitching for the edging, work loosely.
6. See page 113 for a tutorial on Front Post Double Crochet (fpdc), page 114 for Back Post Double Crochet (bpdc), and page 112 for Double Crochet Decrease (dc dec).
7. You can adjust the size of the sweater up or down by switching to a 6.0mm or a 3.0mm hook

Sweater

Using Color A, ch52.

Row 1: Dc in third chain from hook and in each stitch across (50 sts).

Rows 2–4: Turn, ch3, dc in each stitch across (50 sts).

Row 5: Turn, ch3, dc7, (dc, ch1, dc) in next stitch, dc6, (dc, ch1, dc) in next stitch, dc18, (dc, ch1, dc) in next stitch, dc6, (dc, ch1, dc) in next stitch, dc8 (58 sts).

Row 6: Turn, ch3, dc8, (dc, ch1, dc) in next stitch, dc8, (dc, ch1, dc) in next stitch, dc20, (dc, ch1, dc) in next stitch, dc8, (dc, ch1, dc) in next stitch, dc9 (66 sts).

Row 7 Turn, ch3, dc9, (dc, ch1, dc) in next stitch, dc10, (dc, ch1, dc) in next stitch, dc22, (dc, ch1, dc) in next stitch, dc10, (dc, ch1, dc) in next stitch, dc10 (74 sts).

Row 8: Turn, ch3, dc10, (dc, ch1, dc) in next stitch, dc12, (dc, ch1, dc) in next stitch, dc24, (dc, ch1, dc) in next stitch, dc12, (dc, ch1, dc) in next stitch, dc11 (82 sts).

Row 9: Turn, ch3, dc11, (dc, ch1, dc) in next stitch, dc14, (dc, ch1, dc) in next stitch, dc26, (dc, ch1, dc) in next stitch, dc14, (dc, ch1, dc) in next stitch, dc12 (90 sts).

Row 10: Turn, ch3, dc12, (dc, ch1, dc) in next stitch, dc16, (dc, ch1, dc) in next stitch, dc28, (dc, ch1, dc) in next stitch, dc16, (dc, ch1, dc) in next stitch, dc13 (98 sts).

Row 11: Turn, ch3, dc13, (dc, ch1, dc) in next stitch, dc18, (dc, ch1, dc) in next stitch, dc30, (dc, ch1, dc) in next stitch, dc18, (dc, ch1, dc) in next stitch, dc14 (106 sts).

Row 12: Turn, ch3, dc14, (dc, ch1, dc) in next stitch, dc20, (dc, ch1, dc) in next stitch, dc32, (dc, ch1, dc) in next stitch, dc20, (dc, ch1, dc) in next stitch, dc15 (114 sts).

Row 13: Turn, ch3, dc15, (dc, ch1, dc) in next stitch, dc22, (dc, ch1, dc) in next stitch, dc34, (dc, ch1, dc) in next stitch, dc22, (dc, ch1, dc) in next stitch, dc16 (122 sts).

Row 14: Turn, ch3, dc16, (dc, ch1, dc) in next stitch, dc24, (dc, ch1, dc) in next stitch, dc36, (dc, ch1, dc) in next stitch, dc24, (dc, ch1, dc) in next stitch, dc17 (130 sts).

Row 15: This row will join the garment to create the armholes for the sleeves. Turn, ch3, dc17, dc dec (see Notes) using first and second ch1 space of (dc, ch1, dc) created in Row 14 (first armhole created), dc38, dc dec by using third and fourth ch1 space of (dc, ch1, dc) created in Row 14 (second armhole created), dc18 (76 sts).

Row 16: Do not work over the armholes; work on each stitch created in Row 15. Turn, ch3, dc in each stitch across (76 sts).

Row 17: Turn, ch3, dc in each stitch across (76 sts).

Rows 18–23: Repeat Row 17 (76 sts).

Fasten off Color A. Join Color B.

Rows 24–28: Repeat Row 17. Do not cut yarn at end of Row 28.

This is what the sweater will look like after completing Row 28.

Sleeves

Work the pattern for BOTH sleeves

Join Color A to inside of armhole where dc dec was made.

Round 1 Ch3, working in opposite direction of last row, dc in each stitch, sl st to third chain of ch3 to join.

Rounds 2–11: Turn, ch3, dc in each stitch to complete round, sl st to ch3 to join.

Fasten off Color A. Join Color B. Loosely sl st around and join to first sl st.

Fasten off. Weave in ends.

Front Edging

Position garment so last stitch of Row 28 is positioned to bottom right.

The hook is inserted where you will begin the edging. Work from the bottom to the top.

Row 1: Ch1, using the ends of the rows as stitches, with Color B 2sc in each stitch up the side of the garment, stopping at fourth row from top. Do not work over the collar (48 sts).

Row 2: Turn, ch3, *fpdc (see Notes), bpdc (see Notes), repeat from * to complete row.

Row 3: Turn, ch3, *fpdc, bpdc, repeat from* to next to last stitch, dc in last stitch.

Note: The ribbing should line up (fpdc on the previous bpdc and so on). Fasten off. Working on the other side of the garment, join Color B. Work from the bottom to the top.

Row 1: Ch1, using the ends of the rows as stitches, 2sc in each stitch to end (48 sts).

Row 2: Turn, ch3, *fpdc, bpdc, repeat from* to complete row.

Row 3: Turn, ch3, *fpdc, bpdc, repeat from* to next to last stitch, dc in last stitch. The ribbing should line up (fpdc on the previous bpdc and so on).

Row 4: Turn, ch3, dc in each stitch across.

Row 5: Turn, ch3, dc in each stitch across. Fasten off.

(The 2 rows of dc will be behind the opposite side when buttoned.)

Button Loops/Buttons and Final Edging

Join Color B with a slip stitch at bottom of the first (narrower) edging you created. Working toward top of sweater, loosely sl st 5 stitches, ch6, sl st to same stitch (first button loop/hole completed), *sl st 10, ch6, sl st to same stitch, repeat from* 3 more times.

To finish, sl st 2, 3sl st in top corner stitch, sl st around collar, and down opposite side to bottom. Do not work around bottom edge. Fasten off. Weave in ends.

Line up the buttons across from the button loops and sew onto the garment securely with thread and needle.

The buttonholes are actually loops that will slip over the buttons.

Mock Pockets

Locate the tenth row from the bottom of the sweater.

Right Side

Lay the sweater with flaps together in front of you, join Color B a few stitches in from outside folded edge. Loosely sl st 14 stitches. Fasten off.

Left Side

Join Color B 3 stitches from Color A edge. Loosely sl st 14 stitches. Fasten off. Weave in ends.

Top Pocket

Locate row between top 2 buttons. Join Color B on right side and loosely sl st 6 times across the post. Fasten off. Weave in ends.

Mock pockets are a simple way to add dimension to the sweater.

Skill Level: Beginner

Football Cocoon and Hat Set

For all the football fans, this set is a must-have. It is the perfect shower gift as well as a fun way to celebrate a game at home.

Finished Measurements

Cocoon: Length, 20"; Circumference, 16.5"

Hat: Circumference, 12.5"; Height, 5.5"

Yarn

- Lion Brand Hometown USA, super bulky #6 yarn, 100% acrylic (81 yd/5 oz per skein)
  - 2 skeins #135-125 Billings Chocolate (Color A)
  - 1 skein #135-100 New York White (Color B)

Hook and Other Materials

• N-9.0mm hook or size needed to obtain gauge

• Stitch marker (optional)

Gauge

8 sts and 9 rows in sc = 3" square

Notes

1. Cocoon is worked in the round and is joined by a slip stitch until Round 7, when you work continuously in the round.
2. Ch1 at beginning of each round counts as a stitch.
3. When you change yarns, you will carry the old yarn, not fasten it off. That will allow you to simply drop and pick the yarn up later, with no ends to weave in. For a tutorial, see page 117.
4. The football seams are added after the cocoon is finished.
5. The cocoon length can be increased by increasing the finished rows.
6. Hat is worked from the top down. From Round 4 it is worked continuously in the round. If you like, mark the first stitch of the round with a stitch marker for reference.

Cocoon

Using Color A, ch4, sl st to first chain to make a ring.

Round 1: Ch1 (counts as a stitch here and throughout), 5sc in ring, sl st to ch1 to join (6 sts).

Round 2: Ch1, sc in same stitch, 2sc in each stitch to complete round, sl st to ch1 to join (12 sts).

Round 3: Ch1, 2sc in next stitch, *sc, 2sc in next stitch, repeat from* to complete round, sl st to ch1 to join (18 sts).

Round 4: Ch1, sc, 2sc in next stitch, *sc2, 2sc in next stitch, repeat from* to complete round, sl st to ch1 to join (24 sts).

Round 5: Ch1, sc2, 2sc in next stitch, *sc3, 2sc in next stitch, repeat from* to complete round, sl st to ch1 to join (30 sts).

Round 6: Ch1, sc3, 2sc in next stitch, *sc4, 2sc in next stitch, repeat from* to complete round, sl st to ch1 to join (36 sts).

Rounds 7–10: Working continuously in the round, sc in each stitch (36 sts).

Join Color B, drop Color A (see Notes).

Rounds 11–12: Working continuously in the round, sc in each stitch (36 sts).

Fasten off Color B, pick up Color A.

Rounds 13–30: Working continuously in the round, sc in each stitch (36 sts). To finish, sl st to next stitch.

Fasten off. Weave in ends.

Football Seams

With the crochet hook, pull Color B through the third row above the white stripe and the third row from the top. Slip stitch to secure it into place on the inside at both ends. Cut five 6" lengths of Color B. Thread each piece perpendicular to the piece you've already secured, spacing them evenly and centering them. Slip stitch to secure them on each end on the inside. Trim the ends on the inside and football cocoon is complete.

Hat

Using Color A, ch4, sl st to first chain to make a ring.

Round 1: Ch1, 5sc in ring, sl st to ch1 to join (6 sts).

Round 2: Ch1, sc in same stitch, 2sc in each stitch to complete round, sl st to ch1 to join (12 sts).

Round 3: Ch1, 2sc in next stitch, *sc, 2sc in next stitch, repeat from* to complete round, sl st to ch1 to join (18 sts).

Rounds 4–9: Working continuously in the round, sc in each stitch (18 sts).

Join Color B, drop Color A (see Notes).

Rounds 10–11: Working continuously in the round, sc in each stitch (18 sts).

Fasten off Color B, pick up Color A.

Round 12: Working continuously in the round, sc in each stitch (18 sts). To finish, sl st to next stitch.

Fasten off. Weave in ends.

Fruit Punch Hat

Bring in a punch of color with this fun variegated yarn. This hat is a great way to liven up any cold day. To make this delightful project for a boy, just leave off the flower.

Finished Measurements

Newborn: Circumference, 12–14";
  Hat height, 5"

3–6 months: Circumference, 14–17";
  Hat height, 5.5"

9–12 months: Circumference, 16–19";
  Hat height, 6"

Yarn

- Yarn Bee Aurora Borealis Twist, medium worsted weight #4 yarn, 100% cotton (218 yd/3.5 oz per skein)
    1 skein #50 Fruit Punch

Hook and Other Materials
- H-5.0mm hook or size needed to obtain gauge
- Stitch marker (optional)

Gauge
10 sts and 8 rows in dc = 3" square

Notes

1. This hat is worked from the top down in the round.

2. The ch2 at the beginning of each round does not count as a stitch.

3. See page 113 for a tutorial on Front Post Double Crochet (fpdc).

Hat

Newborn

Ch4.

Round 1: 7dc in first chain, sl st to fourth chain of first ch4 to join round (8 sts).

Round 2: Ch2, 2fpdc (see Notes) in each stitch to complete round, sl st to first fpdc to join (16 sts).

Round 3: Ch2, *fpdc, 2fpdc in next stitch, repeat from* to complete round, sl st to first fpdc to join (24 sts).

Round 4: Ch2, *fpdc2, 2fpdc in next stitch, repeat from* to complete round, sl st to first fpdc to join (32 sts).

Rounds 5–14: Ch2, fpdc in each stitch to complete round, sl st to first fpdc to join (32 sts).

Rounds 15–16: Ch1, sc in each stitch to complete round, sl st to ch1 to join (32 sts).

Fasten off. Weave in ends.

3–6 Months

Ch4.

Round 1: 7dc in first chain, sl st to fourth chain of first ch4 to join round (8 sts).

Round 2: Ch2, 2fpdc (see Notes) in each stitch to complete round, sl st to first fpdc to join (16 sts).

Round 3: Ch2, *fpdc, 2fpdc in next stitch, repeat from* to complete round, sl st to first fpdc to join (24 sts).

Round 4: Ch2, *fpdc2, 2fpdc in next stitch, repeat from* to complete round, sl st to first fpdc to join (32 sts).

Round 5: Ch2, *fpdc3, 2fpdc in next stitch, repeat from* to complete round, sl st to first fpdc to join (40 sts).

Rounds 6–18: Ch2, fpdc in each stitch to complete round, sl st to first fpdc to join (40 sts).

Rounds 19–20: Ch1, sc in each stitch to complete round, sl st to ch1 to join (40 sts).

Fasten off. Weave in ends.

9–12 Months

Ch4.

Round 1: 7dc in first chain, sl st to fourth chain of first ch4 to join round (8 sts).

Round 2: Ch2, 2fpdc (see Notes) in each stitch to complete round, sl st to first fpdc to join (16 sts).

Round 3: Ch2, *fpdc, 2fpdc in next stitch, repeat from* to complete round, sl st to first fpdc to join (24 sts).

Round 4: Ch2, *fpdc2, 2fpdc in next stitch, repeat from* to complete round, sl st to first fpdc to join (32 sts).

Round 5: Ch2, *fpdc3, 2fpdc in next stitch, repeat from* to complete round, sl st to first fpdc to join (40 sts).

Round 6: Ch2, *fpdc4, 2fpdc in next stitch, repeat from* to complete round, sl st to first fpdc to join (48 sts).

Rounds 7–22: Ch2, fpdc in each stitch to complete round, sl st to first fpdc to join (48 sts).

Rounds 23–24: Ch1, sc in each stitch to complete round, sl st to ch1 to join (48 sts).

Fasten off. Weave in ends.

Ties (make 2)

Mark the hat evenly on each side for the ties with a stitch marker. For each tie, cut 6 lengths of yarn 3' long. Align the ends, then, holding them together, fold them in half. With a crochet hook, pull the center fold through the marked stitch. Take hold of the cut ends and thread them through the fold. Pull tight on the ends. Working with 3 groups of 4 strands, braid the yarn up to the hat, knot the end, and trim to finish.

Flower

Ch4.

Round 1: 7dc in first chain, sl st to fourth chain of first ch4 to join round (8 sts).

Round 2: Ch2, 2fpdc (see Notes) in each stitch to complete round, sl st to first fpdc to join (16 sts).

Round 3: Ch2, *fpdc, 2fpdc in next stitch, repeat from* to complete round, sl st to first fpdc to join (24 sts).

Round 4: Turn, ch1, *skip 1 stitch, 5dc in next stitch, skip 1 stitch, sl st in next stitch, repeat from* to complete round, sl st to first ch1 to join (24 sts).

Fasten off. Weave in ends.

Attach flower to hat with yarn needle with the spiral side of the center flower facing out.

Who has the cutest baby? You will when he (or she) is wearing this super sweet owl hat!

Finished Measurements

Newborn: Circumference, 12–14";
    Hat height, 5"

3–6 months: Circumference, 14–17";
    Hat height, 5.5"

9–12 months: Circumference, 16–19";
    Hat height, 6"

Yarn

- Red Heart Light & Lofty, super bulky weight #6 yarn, 100% acrylic (105 yd/4.5 oz per skein)

  1 skein #9965 Zebra Stripe (Color A)
- Lion Brand Vanna's Choice Baby, medium worsted weight #4 yarn, 100% acrylic (170 yd/3.5 oz per skein)

  1 skein #840-098 Lamb (Color B)

  1 skein #840-157 Duckie (Color C)

  1 skein #840-132 Goldfish (Color D)

Hook and Other Materials
- N-9.0mm hook or size needed to obtain gauge
- H-5.0mm hook or size needed to obtain gauge
- Stitch marker (optional)
- Yarn needle
- 2 small black buttons
- Sewing thread and needle

Gauge

Using Color A and N-9.0mm hook, 7 sts and 7 rows in sc = 3" square Using Color B, C, or D and H-5.0mm hook, 11 sts and 13 rows in sc = 3" square

Notes

1. The hat is worked from the bottom up continuously in the round. If you like, mark the first stitch of the round with a stitch marker for reference.

2. The eyes, ears, and fringe are made separately and added last.

3. See page 109 for a tutorial on Single Crochet Decrease (sc dec) and page 119 for how to make fringe.

Hat

Newborn

Using Color A and N-9mm hook, ch30, sl st to first chain to create a ring (30 sts).

Round 1: Ch1, sc in each stitch to complete round (30 sts).

Round 2: Working continuously in the round, sc in each stitch (30 sts).

Rounds 3–9: Sc in each stitch (30 sts).

Round 10: 2dc in each stitch (60 sts).

Rounds 11–12: Sc in each stitch (60 sts).

Fasten off, leaving a long tail to sew top of hat together.

3–6 Months
Using Color A and N-9mm hook, ch40, sl st to first chain to create a ring (40 sts).
Round 1: Ch1, sc in each stitch to complete round (40 sts).
Round 2: Working continuously in the round, sc in each stitch (40 sts).
Round 3–12: Sc in each stitch (40 sts).
Round 13: 2dc in each stitch (80 sts).
Rounds 14–15: Sc in each stitch (80 sts).
Fasten off, leaving a long tail to sew top of hat together.

9–12 Months
Using Color A and N-9mm hook, ch50, sl st to first chain to create a ring (50 sts).
Round 1: Ch1, sc in each stitch (50 sts).
Round 2: Working continuously in the round, sc in each stitch (50 sts).
Round 3–15: Sc in each stitch (50 sts) **Round 16:** 2dc in each stitch (100 sts).
Rounds 17–18: Sc in each stitch (100 sts).
Fasten off, leaving a long tail to sew top of hat together.

For All Sizes
Fold the hat in half and use the yarn needle to sew the top of the hat together. The ears will naturally pull to each side.
Fasten off. Weave in ends.

Eyes (make 2 of each)

Back
Using Color B and H-5.0mm hook, ch2.
Round 1: 6sc in first chain (6 sts).
Round 2: Working continuously in the round, 2sc in each stitch (12 sts).
Round 3: *Sc, 2sc in next stitch, repeat from* to complete round (18 sts).
Round 4: *Sc2, 2sc in next stitch, repeat from* to complete round (24 sts).
Round 5: *Sc3, 2sc in next stitch, repeat from* to complete round (32 sts). Sl st to first stitch of round. Fasten off. Weave in ends.

Top

Using Color C and H-5.0mm hook, ch2.

Round 1: 6sc in first chain (6 sts).

Round 2: Working continuously in the round, 2sc in each stitch (12 sts).

Round 3: *Sc, 2sc in next stitch, repeat from* to complete round (18 sts). Sl st to first stitch of round.

Fasten off. Weave in ends.

Beak

Using Color D and H-5.0mm hook, ch6.

Row 1: Turn, sc in first chain from hook and across (5 sts).

Row 2: Turn, sc in each stitch (5 sts).

Row 3: Turn, sc, sc dec (see Notes), use middle stitch again and sc dec, sc (4 sts).

Row 4: Turn, sc dec, sc dec (2 sts).

Row 5: Turn, sc dec, ch1 (1 st).

Fasten off, leaving a long tail to sew onto hat.

Finishing

Using yarn needle, sew the back eyes onto the hat, followed by the top eyes. With the sewing needle, sew the buttons onto the top eyes as preferred (looking up, down, sideways, cross-eyed, etc.). Using the yarn needle, sew the beak in the center below the eyes. Fasten off. Weave in all ends.

Fringe on Ears

Cut three 4" lengths each of Colors B and C and add as you would fringe (see Notes) to each ear. Trim to same length.

Vivianne Slippers

Don't be intimidated by this simple slipper. It is easy to create but looks amazing when finished.

Finished Measurements
Newborn: Toe to heel, 2.5"
3–6 months: Toe to heel, 3"
9–12 months: Toe to heel, 3.5"

Yarn

- Peaches & Crème, worsted weight #4 yarn, 100% cotton (120 yd/2.5 oz per skein)

    1 skein #1712 Bright Lime
    1 skein #1740 Bright Pink

Hook and Other Materials
• E-3.5mm hook or size needed to obtain gauge

Gauge

15 sts and 15 rows in sc = 3" square

Notes

1. The soles of the shoe are made first, sewn together, and the top section added last.
2. Do not count the ch1 or sl st as a stitch.
3. See page 110 for tutorial on Half Double Crochet (hdc) and page 107 for working back loop only (blo) of a stitch.
4. The flower is optional.

Special Technique
Double Treble Crochet (dbtr)

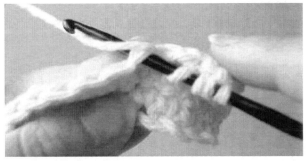

1. Yarn over 3 times, push hook through stitch.

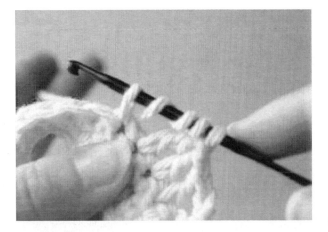

2. Yarn over, pull back through: 5 stitches on hook.

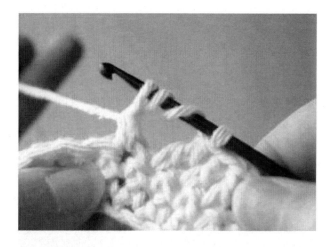

3. Yarn over, pull through first 2 stitches: 4 stitches on hook.

4. Yarn over, pull through first 2 stitches: 3 stitches on hook.

5. Yarn over, pull through first 2 stitches: 2 stitches on hook.

6. Yarn over, pull through last 2 stitches: Double Treble is complete.

Sole (make 2 in each color)

Newborn

Ch7.

Round 1: Turn, sc5, dc6 in last chain, working on opposite side of chain sc5, sl st to first sc on other side of chain to join (16 sts).

Round 2: Ch1, 2sc in same stitch, sc4, 2hdc (see Notes) in next stitch, hdc, 2hdc in next 2 stitches, hdc, 2hdc in next stitch, sc5, sl st to ch1 to join (21 sts).

Round 3: Ch1, 2sc in next 2 stitches, sc5, *2sc in next stitch, sc, repeat from* 3 more times, 2sc in next stitch, sc5, sl st to ch1 to join (28 sts).

Fasten off, leaving a long tail on both of the soles of one color to use to sew the soles together.

3–6 Months

Ch9.

Round 1: Turn, sc7, dc6 in last chain, working on opposite side of chain sc7, sl st to first sc on other side of chain to join (20 sts).

Round 2: Ch1, 2sc in same stitch, sc6, 2hdc (see Notes) in next stitch, hdc, 2hdc in next 2 stitches, hdc, 2hdc in next stitch, sc7, sl st to ch1 to join (25 sts).

Round 3: Ch1, 2sc in next 2 stitches, sc7, *2sc in next stitch, sc, repeat from* 3 more times, 2sc in next stitch, sc7, sl st to ch1 to join (32 sts).

Fasten off, leaving a long tail on both of the soles of one color to use to sew the soles together.

9–12 Months

Ch12.

Round 1: Turn, sc10, dc6 in last chain, working on opposite side of chain sc10, sl st to first sc on other side of chain to join (26 sts).

Round 2: Ch1, 2sc in same stitch, sc9, 2hdc (see <u>Notes</u>) in next stitch, hdc, 2hdc in next 2 stitches, hdc, 2hdc in next stitch, sc10, sl st to ch1 to join (31sts).

Round 3: Ch1, 2sc in next 2 stitches, sc10, *2sc, sc, repeat from* 3 more times, 2sc in next stitch, sc10, sl st to ch1 to join (38 sts).

Fasten off, leaving a long tail on both of the soles of one color to use to sew the soles together.

With wrong sides facing, use the yarn needle to sew 2 soles of different colors together. Simply weave in and out of the last round.

If you use two colors, this is how the bottom of the shoe will look when sewn together.

Sides and Top

Newborn

Join Color A at last sl st on the Color B sole.

Round 1: Ch1, sc in each stitch using blo (see <u>Notes</u>) to complete round, sl st to ch1 to join (28 sts).

Round 2: Ch1, sc in each stitch to complete round, sl st to ch1 to join (28 sts).

Round 3: Ch1, sc5, ch4, dbtr (see Special Technique, pages <u>88–89</u>) in next stitch leaving last loop on the hook (see Photo 1 below), *skip a stitch, dbtr in next stitch leaving last loop on hook, repeat from* 6 more times (total of 8 dbtr; see <u>Photo 2</u> below), yarn over, pull yarn through all loops on hook (see Photo 3 on <u>page 91</u>), sl st, ch4. From outside of shoe, sc to join ch4 to next stitch (see <u>Photo 4</u>), sc10 to complete round, sl st to ch1 to join.

1. Here you can see the ch4 and double treble. Leave the last loop of each double treble on the hook. Skip a stitch and repeat until you have 8 dbtr.

2. Here you see the double trebles and the last loop of each double treble on the hook.

3. Yarn over and pull through all the loops on hook. Sl st.

4. Ch4, sc to next stitch. Follow the pattern to complete Round 3.

Round 4: Ch1, sc4, ch6, sc in next stitch on opposite side, sc7 around back of shoe to complete round, sl st to ch1 to join.

Fasten off. Weave in ends.

3–6 Months|

Join Color A at last sl st on Color B sole.

Round 1: Ch1, sc in each stitch using blo (see <u>Notes</u>) to complete round, sl st to ch1 to join (32 sts).

Round 2: Ch1, sc in each stitch to complete round, sl st to ch1 to join (32 sts).

Round 3: Ch1, sc7, ch4, dbtr (see Special Technique on pages <u>88–89</u>) in next stitch leaving last loop on hook (see Photo 1 on <u>page 90</u>), *skip a stitch, dbtr in next stitch leaving last loop on the hook, repeat from* 6 more times (total of 8 dbtr; see Photo 2 on <u>page 90</u>), yarn over, pull yarn through all loops on hook, sl st, ch4 (see <u>Photo 3</u> above left). From outside of shoe, sc to join ch4 to next stitch (see Photo 4 left), sc12 to complete round, sl st to ch1 to join. Round 4: Ch1, sc6, ch6, sc in next stitch on opposite side, sc8 around back of shoe to complete round, sl st to ch1 to join.

Fasten off. Weave in ends.

9–12 Months

Join Color A at last sl st on Color B sole.

Round 1: Ch1, sc in each stitch using blo (see Notes) to complete round, sl st to ch1 to join (38 sts).

Round 2: Ch1, sc in each stitch to complete round, sl st to ch1 to join (38 sts).

Round 3: Ch1, sc10, ch4, dbtr (see Special Technique on pages 88–89) in next stitch leaving last loop on hook (see Photo 1 on page 90), *skip a stitch, dbtr in next stitch leaving last loop on hook, repeat from* 6 more times (total of 8 dbtr; see Photo 2 on page 90), yarn over, pull yarn through all loops on hook, sl st, ch4 (see Photo 3 above left). From outside of shoe, sc to join ch4 to next stitch (see Photo 4 left), sc14 to complete round, sl st to ch1 to join.

Round 4: Ch1, sc9, ch6, sc in next stitch on opposite side, sc12 around back of shoe to complete round, sl st to ch1 to join.

Fasten off. Weave in ends.

Flower (make 2; optional)

Using Color A, ch4, sl st to first chain to create a ring.

Round 1: Ch1, 6sc in ring, sl st to ch1 to join (6 sts).

Fasten off Color A.

Round 2: Join Color B with a sl st, *(ch1, 2dc in next stitch, ch1), sl st to same stitch, sl st to next stitch, repeat from* in each stitch to complete petals, sl st to first ch1 to join.

Fasten off. Using yarn needle, attach to top or side of each shoe. Weave in all ends.

Perfect for boys or girls, this giraffe set is a must-make!

Finished Measurements

Hat

Newborn: Circumference, 12–14";
    Hat height, 5.5–6"

3–6 months: Circumference, 14–17";
    Hat height, 6.5–7"

9–12 months: Circumference, 16–19";
    Hat height, 7.5"

Button Diaper Cover
Newborn: Waist, 12"
3–6 months: Waist, 14"
9–12 months: Waist, 16"

Yarn

- Red Heart Super Saver, medium worsted weight #4 yarn, 100% acrylic (364 yd/7 oz per skein)

    1 skein #0320 Cornmeal (Color A)
    1 skein #0365 Coffee (Color B)
    1 skein #0336 Warm Brown (Color C)

Hook and Other Materials

- H-5.0mm hook or size needed to obtain gauge
- Stitch markers
- Yarn needle
- Two 1" black buttons
- Sewing thread and needle

Gauge
11 sts and 14 rows in sc = 4" square

Hat Notes

1. The hat is worked from the top down continuously in the round. If you like, mark the first stitch of the round with a stitch marker for your reference.
2. The gauge should be loose for this pattern, so please check before beginning.
3. The eyes, ears, and horns will be added to the hat separately. The foundation row of the nose is crocheted right onto the hat and then the rest is sewn on.
4. See page 109 for a tutorial on Single Crochet Decrease (sc dec) and page 112 for Double Crochet Decrease (dc dec).

Button Diaper Cover Notes

1. The diaper cover is a single panel worked front to back. A strip will be attached to the back section.
2. After the main panel is made, the trimming is added in Color B.

Hat

Newborn

Using Color A, ch4, sl st to first chain to create a ring.

Round 1: Ch1 (this counts as your first sc), 7sc in ring (8 sts).

Round 2: Working continuously in the round, 2sc in each stitch (16 sts).

Round 3: *Sc, 2sc in next stitch, repeat from* to complete round (24 sts).

Round 4: *Sc2, 2sc in next stitch, repeat from* to complete round (32 sts).

Rounds 5–16: Sc in each stitch (32 sts). To finish, sl st to first stitch of round. Fasten off. Weave in ends.

3–6 Months

Using Color A, ch4, sl st to first chain to create a ring.

Round 1: Ch1 (this counts as your first sc), 7sc in ring (8 sts).

Round 2: Working continuously in the round, 2sc in each stitch (16 sts).

Round 3: *Sc, 2sc in next stitch, repeat from* to complete round (24 sts).

Round 4: *Sc2, 2sc in next stitch, repeat from* to complete round (32 sts).

Round 5: *Sc3, 2sc in next stitch, repeat from* to complete round (40 sts).

Rounds 6–20: Sc in each stitch (40 sts). To finish, sl st to first stitch of round. Fasten off. Weave in ends.

9–12 Months

Using Color A, ch4, sl st to first chain to create a ring.

Round 1: Ch1 (this counts as your first sc), 7sc in ring (8 sts).

Round 2: Working continuously in the round, 2sc in each stitch (16 sts).

Round 3: *Sc, 2sc in next stitch, repeat from* to complete round (24 sts).

Round 4: *Sc2, 2sc in next stitch, repeat from* to complete round (32 sts).

Round 5: *Sc3, 2sc in next stitch, repeat from* to complete round (40 sts).

Round 6: *Sc4, 2sc in next stitch, repeat from* to complete round (48 sts).

Rounds 7–24: Sc in each stitch (48 sts). To finish, sl st to first stitch of round. Fasten off. Weave in ends.

Nose

Join Color C in any stitch on the last row.

Row 1: Ch1, sc 18 (18 sts).

Row 2: Turn, ch1, sc18 (18 sts).

Row 3: Turn, ch1, sc 18 (18 sts).

Row 4: Turn, sc dec (see Notes), sc14, sc dec (16 sts).

Row 5: Turn, sc dec, sc12, sc dec (14 sts).

Row 6: Turn, sc dec, sc 10; sc dec (12 sts).

Fasten off, leaving a long tail to sew the nose down to the hat.

Flip the panel up onto the hat, and with yarn needle, sew all around the nose to secure it in place.

Nose Holes (make 2)

Using Color B, ch2.

Round 1: Sc6 in first chain. Sl st to first stitch to join (6 sts).

Fasten off, leaving a long tail to sew onto nose.

Horns (make 2)

Using Color B, ch2.

Round 1: Sc4 in first chain (4 sts).

Round 2: Working continuously in the round, 2sc in each stitch (8 sts).

Round 3: *Sc, 2sc in next stitch, repeat from* to complete round (12 sts).

Rounds 4–5: Sc12 (12 sts).

Round 6: *Sc, sc dec, repeat from* to complete round (9 sts).

Fasten off Color B, join Color A.

Rounds 7–12: Sc 9 (9 sts). To finish, sl st to first stitch of round.

Fasten off, leaving a long tail to sew horns onto hat.

Ears (make 2)

Using Color A, ch4.

Round 1: 4dc in first chain from hook, sl st to third chain to join round (5 sts).

Round 2: Ch3 (counts as first dc here and throughout), dc in same stitch, 2dc in next stitch and to complete round, sl st to third chain of ch3 to join (10 sts).

Round 3: Ch3, 2dc in next stitch, *dc, 2dc in next stitch, repeat from* to complete round, sl st to third chain of ch3 to join (15 sts).

Round 4: Ch3, dc in each stitch and to complete round, sl st to third chain of first ch3 to join (15 sts).

Round 5: Ch3, dc dec (see Notes), *dc, dc dec, repeat from* to complete round, sl st to third chain of first ch3 to join (10 sts).

Round 6: Ch3, dc dec, *dc, dc dec, repeat from* to next to last stitch, dc in last stitch, sl st to third chain of first ch3 to join round (7 sts).

Fasten off, leaving a long tail to sew ear onto hat.

Finishing

Using yarn needle, sew the horns onto hat 1 row down from the top center. Sew the ears next to the horns and the nose holes onto the nose. Next, using the sewing needle and thread, securely sew the buttons on for the eyes. Weave in all ends.

Button Diaper Cover

Newborn

Using Color A, ch19.

Row 1: Sc in first chain from hook and across (18 sts).

Row 2: Turn, ch1, sc in each stitch (18 sts).

Rows 3–9: Repeat Row 2.

Row 10: Turn, sc dec (see Notes), sc14, sc dec (16 sts).

Row 11: Turn, sc dec, sc12, sc dec (14 sts).

Row 12: Turn, sc dec, sc10, sc dec (12 sts).

Row 13: Turn, sc dec, sc8, sc dec (10 sts).

Rows 14–26: Turn, ch1, sc in each stitch (10 sts).

Row 27: Turn, ch1, sc in same stitch, sc8, 2sc in last stitch (12 sts).

Row 28: Turn, ch1, sc in same stitch, sc10, 2sc in last stitch (14 sts).

Row 29: Turn, ch1, sc in same stitch, sc12, 2sc in last stitch (16 sts).

Row 30: Turn, ch1, sc in same stitch, sc14, 2sc in last stitch (18 sts).

Rows 31–33: Turn, ch1, sc in each stitch (18 sts).

Fasten off. Weave in ends.

Top Strip

Using Color A, ch10.

Row 1: Sc in same stitch just fastened off on diaper cover, sc17, ch11 (38 sts).

Row 2: Turn, sc in first chain from hook and across (37 sts).
Rows 3–5: Turn, ch1, sc in each stitch (37 sts).
Fasten off. Weave in ends.

3–6 Months

Using Color A, ch21.
Row 1: Sc in first chain from hook and across (20 sts).
Row 2: Turn, ch1, sc in each stitch (20 sts).
Rows 3–11: Repeat Row 2.
Row 12: Turn, sc dec (see Notes), sc16, sc dec (18 sts).
Row 13: Turn, sc dec, sc14, sc dec (16 sts).
Row 14: Turn, sc dec, sc12, sc dec (14 sts).
Row 15: Turn, sc dec, sc10, sc dec (12 sts).
Rows 16–28: Turn, ch1, sc in each stitch (12 sts).
Row 29: Turn, ch1, sc in same stitch, sc10, 2sc in last stitch (14 sts).
Row 30: Turn, ch1, sc in same stitch, sc12, 2sc in last stitch (16 sts).
Row 31: Turn, ch1, sc in same stitch, sc14, 2sc in last stitch (18 sts).
Row 32: Turn, ch1, sc in same stitch, sc16, 2sc in last stitch (20 sts).
Rows 33–35: Turn, ch1, sc in each stitch (20 sts).
Fasten off. Weave in ends

Top Strip

Using Color A, ch12.
Row 1: Sc in same stitch just fastened off on diaper cover, sc19, ch13 (44 sts).
Row 2: Turn, sc in first chain from hook and across (43 sts).
Rows 3–5: Turn, ch1, sc in each stitch (43 sts).
Fasten off. Weave in ends.

9–12 Months

Using Color A, ch25.
Row 1: Sc in first chain and across (24 sts).
Row 2: Turn, ch1, sc in each stitch (24 sts).
Rows 3–13: Repeat Row 2.
Row 14: Turn, sc dec (see Notes), sc20, sc dec (22 sts).
Row 15: Turn, sc dec, sc18, sc dec (20 sts).
Row 16: Turn, sc dec, sc16, sc dec (18 sts).
Row 17: Turn, sc dec, sc14, sc dec (16 sts).
Rows 18–30: Turn, ch1, sc in each stitch (16 sts).
Row 31: Turn, ch1, sc in same stitch, sc14, 2sc in last stitch (18 sts).

Row 32: Turn, ch1, sc in same stitch, sc16, 2sc in last stitch (20 sts).
Row 33: Turn, ch1, sc in same stitch, sc18, 2sc in last stitch (22 sts).
Row 34: Turn, ch1, sc in same stitch, sc20, 2sc in last stitch (24 sts).
Rows 35–37: Turn, ch1, sc in each stitch (24 sts).
Fasten off. Weave in ends.

Top Strip
Using Color A, ch15.
Row 1: Sc in same stitch just fastened off on diaper cover, sc23, ch16 (54 sts).
Row 2: Turn, sc in first chain from hook and across (53 sts).
Rows 3–5: Turn, ch1, sc in each stitch (53 sts).
Fasten off. Weave in ends.

Trim (for all sizes)

Join Color B at the top right corner of the strip.
Round 1: Ch1, using ends of rows as stitches, sc in each stitch around, with the exception of the 4 corners of the strip and 2 corners on front side. In each corner (sc, ch1, sc) in that stitch. Sl st to ch1 to join round.
Fasten off. Weave in ends.

Finishing (for all sizes)

Sew button onto center of front panel. Slip ends of each side of the strip over the button through the stitches.

Cuddle Me Hat and Cocoon Set

Let your newborn snuggle up and drift off to a peaceful sleep in this sweet cocoon set.

Finished Measurements
Newborn
Cocoon: Circumference, 16";
    Length, 16.5"
Hat: Circumference, 12.5";
    Height, 5.5"
(For other sizes, see Notes.) **Yarn**
• Patons Melody Quick & Cozy, super bulky #6 yarn, 100% acrylic (72 yd/3.5 oz per skein)

3 skeins #19733 Pinky Girl

Hook and Other Materials

• N-9.0mm hook or size needed to obtain gauge • Stitch marker (optional)
• Yarn needle

Gauge
7 sts and 5 rows in dc = 4" square

Hat Notes
1. The hat is worked from the top down continuously in the round. If you like, mark the beginning of the round with a stitch marker for reference.
2. If extra length is needed, add more rounds; this hat stretches easily, so additional length is really only needed for an older baby.

Cocoon Notes
1. The cocoon is made in 1 piece, sewn two-thirds of the way up, and then joined at the bottom to finish.
2. Ch3 in each row counts as a dc.
3. If the cocoon needs extra length, add more rows.

4. See page 120 for a photo tutorial for a basic sewing stitch.

Hat

Ch4.

Round 1: 10dc in first chain, sl st to first dc stitch to join (10 sts).

Round 2: Ch3, dc in same stitch, 2dc in next stitch and to complete round, sl st to ch3 to join (20 sts).

Rounds 3–7: Working continuously in the round, dc in each stitch (20 sts). To finish, sl st to first stitch of next round.

Fasten off. Weave in ends.

Cocoon

Ch32.

Row 1: Turn, dc in fourth chain from hook and in each chain across (30 sts).

Row 2: Turn, ch3 (counts as first dc here and throughout), dc in each stitch across (30 sts).

Rows 3–20: Repeat Row 2.

Fasten off and weave in ends.

Finishing

Fold the panel in half side to side and, using the yarn needle, sew two-thirds of the way up the cocoon with a basic stitch (see Notes). Fasten off and weave in ends. To finish, weave the yarn needle through the edges of the end of the cocoon and pull tight to cinch close. Fasten off and weave in ends.

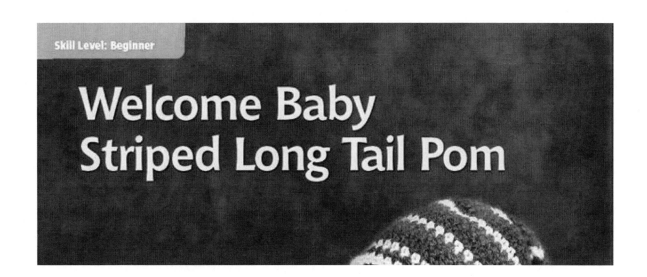

Welcome Baby
Striped Long Tail Pom

Bring your newborn home in this sweet sleeping hat.

Finished Measurements

Newborn: Circumference, 12–14"; Hat height, 5.5–6"

Yarn

- Lion Brand Jiffy, bulky weight #5 yarn (135 yd/3 oz per skein)
  - 1 skein #450-126 Espresso (Color A)
  - 1 skein #450-098 Oat (Color B)
  - 1 skein #450-134 Avocado (Color C)

Hook and Other Materials

• H-5.0mm hook or size needed to obtain gauge
• Stitch marker

Gauge
9 sts and 12 rows in sc = 3" square

Notes

1. The hat is worked from the top down continuously in the round. If you like, mark the first stitch of the round with a stitch marker for your reference.
2. The hat can be worked in a single color or with stripes, as directed here.
3. When making the stripes, you will carry the yarn, not fasten it off, when changing colors for the stripes. See page 117 for a tutorial.
4. See page 120 for a tutorial on how to make a pom.

Hat

With Color A, ch6, sl st to first chain to create a ring.
Round 1: Ch1, sc in each chain (6 sts).
Rounds 2–3: Working continuously in the round, sc in each stitch (6 sts).
Join Color B, drop Color A (do not cut; see Note 3).
Round 4: Sc in each stitch (6 sts).
Join Color C, drop Color B (do not cut).
Rounds 5–6: Sc in each stitch (6 sts).
*Pick up Color A, drop Color C.
Rounds 7–8: Sc in each stitch (6 sts).
Pick up Color B, drop Color A.
Round 9: Sc in each stitch (6 sts).
Pick up Color C, drop Color B.
Rounds 10–11: Sc in each stitch (6 sts).
Rounds 12–45: Repeat from * to complete the "tail" of the hat.
Pick up Color A, drop Color C.|
Round 46: 2sc in each stitch (12 sts).

Round 47: *Sc, 2sc in next stitch, repeat from* to complete round (18 sts).
Pick up Color B, drop Color A.

Round 48: *Sc2, 2sc in next stitch, repeat from* to complete round (24 sts).
Pick up Color C, drop Color B.

Round 49: *Sc3, 2sc in next stitch, repeat from* to complete round (30 sts).

Round 50: *Sc4, 2sc in next stitch, repeat from* to complete round (36 sts).
Pick up Color A, drop Color C.

Rounds 51–52: Sc in each stitch (36 sts).
Pick up Color B, drop Color A.

Round 53: Sc in each stitch (36 sts).
Pick up Color C, drop Color B.

Rounds 54–55: Sc in each stitch (36 sts).
Pick up Color A, drop Color C.

Rounds 56–57: Sc in each stitch (36 sts).
Pick up Color B, drop Color A.

Round 58: Sc in each stitch (36 sts).
Pick up Color A, drop Color B.

Round 59: Sc in each stitch (36 sts).
Pick up Color B, drop Color A.

Round 60: Sc in each stitch (36 sts).

Pick up Color A, drop Color B.
Round 61: Sc in each stitch (36 sts).
Fasten off. Weave in ends.

Finishing

Make a pom (see Notes) and attach to the end of the tail.

Skill Level: Beginner

Cotton Candy Hat

Cotton candy is sweet to eat, but it's even sweeter when worn! This hat will perk up any outfit.

Finished Measurements

Newborn: Circumference, 12–14";
      Hat height, 5.5–6"
3–6 months: Circumference, 14–17";
      Hat height, 6.5–7"
9–12 months: Circumference, 16–19";
      Hat height, 7.5"

Yarn

- Yarn Bee Melody, bulky weight #5 yarn, 70% wool/30% acrylic (129 yd/4 oz per skein)
    - 1 skein #102 Floral (Color A)
- Red Heart Super Saver, medium worsted weight #4 yarn, 100% acrylic (364 yd/7 oz per skein)
    - 1 skein #718 Shocking Pink (Color B)
    - 1 skein #512 Turqua (Color C)

Hook and Other Materials

• H-5.0mm hook or size needed to obtain gauge • Stitch marker (optional)

• Medium button

• Sewing thread and needle

Gauge

Using Color A, 6 sts and 8 rows in sc = 2" square **Notes**

1. The hat is worked from the top down continuously in the round. If you like, mark the first stitch of the round with a stitch marker for reference.
2. The flowers will slip over the button and are removable.

Hat

Newborn

Using Color A, ch4, sl st to first chain to create a ring.

Round 1: Ch1 (this counts as your first sc), 7sc in ring (8 sts).

Round 2: Working continuously in the round, 2sc in each stitch (16 sts).

Round 3: *Sc, 2sc in next stitch, repeat from* to complete round (24 sts).

Round 4: *Sc2, 2sc in next stitch, repeat from* to complete round (32 sts).

Rounds 5–16: Sc in each stitch (32 sts). To finish, sl st to first stitch of round.

Fasten off. Weave in ends.

3–6 Months
Using Color A, ch4, sl st to first chain to create a ring.
Round 1: Ch1 (this counts as your first sc), 7sc in ring (8 sts).
Round 2: Working continuously in the round, 2sc in each stitch (16 sts).
Round 3: *Sc, 2sc in next stitch, repeat from* to complete round (24 sts).
Round 4: *Sc2, 2sc in next stitch, repeat from* to complete round (32 sts).
Round 5: *Sc3, 2sc in next stitch, repeat from* to complete round (40 sts).
Rounds 6–20: Sc in each stitch (40 sts). To finish, sl st to first stitch of round.
Fasten off. Weave in ends.

9–12 Months
Using Color A, ch4, sl st to first chain to create a ring.
Round 1: Ch1 (this counts as your first sc), 7sc in ring (8 sts).
Round 2: Working continuously in the round, 2sc in each stitch (16 sts).
Round 3: *Sc, 2sc in next stitch, repeat from* to complete round (24 sts).
Round 4: *Sc2, 2sc in next stitch, repeat from* to complete round (32 sts).
Round 5: *Sc3, 2sc in next stitch, repeat from* to complete round (40 sts).
Round 6: *Sc4, 2sc in next stitch, repeat from* to complete round (48 sts).
Rounds 7–24: Sc in each stitch (48 sts). To finish, sl st to first stitch of round.
Fasten off. Weave in ends.

Back Flower
Using Color C, ch4, sl st to first chain to create a ring.
Round 1: 9sc in ring, sl st to first stitch to join round (9 sts).
Round 2: *Ch10, sl st in same stitch, ch10, sl st in same stitch, sl st in next stitch, repeat from* to complete round.
Fasten off. Weave in ends.

Top Flower
Using Color B, ch4, sl st to first chain to create a ring.
Round 1: 9sc in ring, sl st to first stitch to join round (9 sts).
Round 2: *Ch6, sl st in same stitch, ch6, sl st in same stitch, sl st in next stitch, repeat from* to complete round.
Fasten off. Weave in ends.

Finishing

With sewing needle and thread, sew the button onto hat. Slip centers of flowers over button.

 # How to Read My Patterns

Skill Level

To help you pick a pattern that is consistent with your crochet experience, every pattern in the book indicates its skill level: beginner, intermediate, or advanced. For patterns designated for beginners, you'll need to know how to chain, single crochet, half double crochet, and/or double crochet. As you move up the skill level ladder, more stitch knowledge is required, but there are photo tutorials included in this book for every single stitch you'll need to know. And none of the patterns are difficult. My design goal is always to create the sweetest items using the simplest stitches possible.

If you are a novice crocheter, let me recommend that you start with Cream Puff Hat (page 40), Football Cocoon and Hat Set (page 80), or Cotton Candy Hat (page 100). These patterns will allow you to practice and perfect the basics before moving onto other stitches and techniques.

Yarn

Under Yarn, you will find listed the specific yarn(s) and colors I used to crochet the pattern, plus how many skeins you'll need. Also included is that specific yarn's "yarn weight." You'll find this information on the label of every skein of yarn you buy, and it ranges from #0 lace weight to #6 super bulky weight. If you can't find the specific yarn I use or you'd like to use something else, knowing the yarn weight will let you pick another yarn that will have the same gauge.

Standard Yarn Weight System

Categories of yarn, gauge ranges, and recommended needle and hook sizes

Yarn Weight Symbol & Category Names	0 LACE	1 SUPER FINE	2 FINE	3 LIGHT	4 MEDIUM	5 BULKY	6 SUPER BULKY
Type of Yarns in Category	Fingering 10-count crochet thread	Sock, Fingering, Baby	Sport, Baby	DK, Light Worsted	Worsted, Afghan, Aran	Chunky, Craft, Rug	Bulky, Roving
Knit Gauge Range* in Stockinette Stitch to 4 inches	33–40** sts	27–32 sts	23–26 sts	21–24 st	16–20 sts	12–15 sts	6–11 sts
Recommended Needle in Metric Size Range	1.5–2.25 mm	2.25–3.25 mm	3.25–3.75 mm	3.75–4.5 mm	4.5–5.5 mm	5.5–8 mm	8 mm and larger
Recommended Needle U.S. Size Range	000–1	1 to 3	3 to 5	5 to 7	7 to 9	9 to 11	11 and larger
Crochet Gauge* Ranges in Single Crochet to 4 inch	32–42 double crochets**	21–32 sts	16–20 sts	12–17 sts	11–14 sts	8–11 sts	5–9 sts
Recommended Hook in Metric Size Range	Steel*** 1.6–1.4 mm	2.25–3.5 mm	3.5–4.5 mm	4.5–5.5 mm	5.5–6.5 mm	6.5–9 mm	9 mm and larger
Recommended Hook U.S. Size Range	Steel*** 6, 7, 8 Regular hook B–1	B–1 to E–4	E–4 to 7	7 to I–9	I–9 to K–10 1/2	K–10 1/2 to M–13	M–13 and larger

*GUIDELINES ONLY: The above reflect the most commonly used gauges and needle or hook sizes for specific yarn categories.

**Lace weight yarns are usually knitted or crocheted on larger needles and hooks to create lacy, openwork patterns. Accordingly, a gauge range is difficult to determine. Always follow the gauge stated in your pattern.

***Steel crochet hooks are sized differently from regular hooks—the higher the number, the smaller the hook, which is the reverse of regular hook sizing.

Source: Craft Yarn Council of America's www.YarnStandards.com

Source: Craft Yarn Council of America's www.YarnStandards.com

Hooks and Other Materials Here you'll find the hook sizes you'll need, plus any additional materials or tools, which most commonly will include stitch markers, a yarn needle, and a sewing needle and thread.

Gauge

The key to crocheting a garment that fits is to check gauge. Every pattern in this book tells you the gauge for that project, namely how many stitches and rows per inch the final measurements (and final fit) were based on.

To check gauge, you need to crochet a sample swatch using the yarn, hook size, and crochet stitch called for. Crochet the swatch at least 1" larger than required so that you can check the stitches and rows within the swatch to ensure proper gauge. For instance, if the gauge is determined to be 3" square in single crochet, you will work up a swatch in single crochet at least 4" square. Lay a measuring tape on the swatch and count across how many stitches you have in 3". Now reposition the tape and measure up and down how many rows you have in 3".

If you have more stitches and rows than you should, try the next larger hook size, and make another gauge swatch. Keep doing this until the swatch matches the pattern gauge. If you have fewer stitches and rows than you should, retest your gauge with the next size smaller hook in same way.

Notes

Be sure to read the Notes section before beginning a project. You'll find helpful hints there, including what stitches beyond the basic single crochet and double crochet might be used and cross references to tutorials for them.

Special Techniques

A few of the patterns include stitch tutorials, which you'll find under Special Techniques. In most cases, these stitches are particular to that specific pattern.

Directions

• When.3 a number is before the command, such as 3hdc, you will work in the SAME stitch.

• When a number is after the command, such as hdc3, you will work that command in that number of following stitches.

• The number in parentheses at the end of a round or row is the TOTAL number of stitches for that round or row.

• The asterisks will mark a specific placement in a pattern that will be used when repeating sections.

• Working "in the round" means that you will be working in one direction throughout, not back and forth in rows. To work "continuously in the round" means that the rounds will be crocheted without joining.

• When you see commands written within a set of parentheses, all those commands will be crocheted in the same stitch, for example "(ch1, dc, ch1) in the next stitch."

Abbreviations

blo	back loop only
ch	chain
dc	double crochet
dc dec	double crochet decrease
dec	decrease
dbtr	double treble crochet
flo	front loop only
hdc	half double crochet
hdc dec	half double crochet decrease
inc	increase
sc	single crochet
sc dec	single crochet decrease
sk	skip
sl st	slip stitch
sl st dec	slip stitch decrease
st(s)	stitch(es)
tr	treble crochet

 **Stitch Guide**

Here you will find everything you need to know to crochet the patterns in this book, even if you've never picked up a crochet hook before.

How to Hold a Crochet Hook

There are two ways to hold a hook; use the one that's more comfortable for you.

Over the Hook Hold

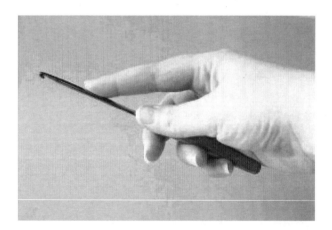

Place your hand over the hook with the handle resting against the palm and thumb and your index finger on the thumb rest.

Under the Hook Hold

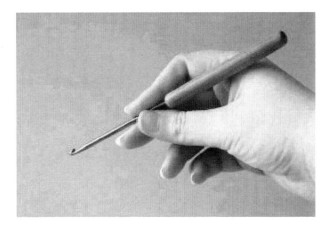

Hold the hook in your hand as you would hold a pencil between your thumb and forefinger.

How to Hold Yarn

As with holding the hook, there are several different ways to hold the yarn when crocheting. Choose the one that is most comfortable. Pay attention to tension, which is how tightly you are pulling on the yarn. You want to maintain an even tension, which will yield a fabric with evenly sized stitches, not too loose and not too tight.

Over the Pinkie Hold

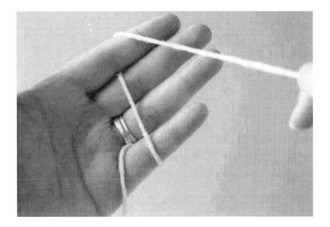

Wrap the yarn over the hand and around your pinkie.

Over the Middle Finger Hold

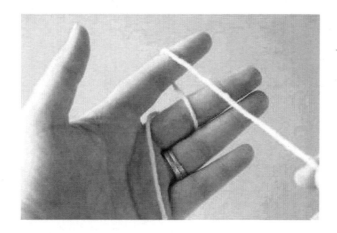

Wrap the yarn around the middle finger and over the forefinger to guide the yarn.

Over the Forefinger Hold

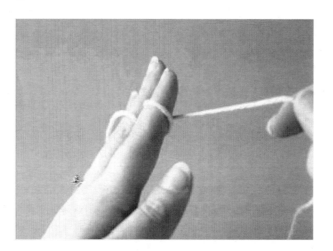

Wrap the yarn around the forefinger.

Slip Knot

This adjustable knot will begin every crochet project.

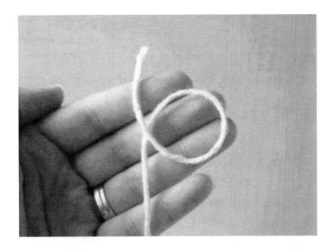

1. Make a loop in the yarn.

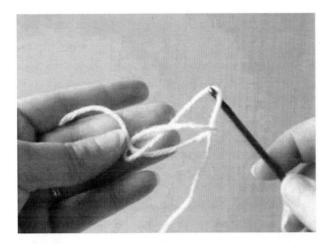

2. With your crochet hook or finger, grab the yarn from the skein and pull through the loop.

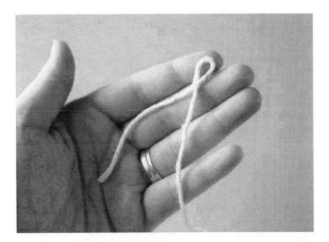

3. Pull tight on the yarn and adjust to create the first loop.

Chain (ch)

The chain provides the foundation for your stitches at the beginning of a pattern. It can also serve as a stitch within a pattern and can be used to create an open effect.

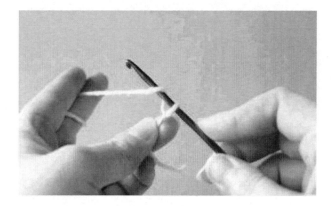

1. Insert the hook through the slip knot, and place the yarn over the hook by passing the hook in front of the yarn.

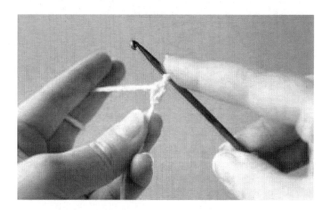

2. Keeping the yarn taut (but not too tight; see Tip below), pull the hook back through the loop with the yarn. Chain 1 is complete.

3. Repeat Steps 1 and 2 to create multiple chains. Tip: Keep chains loose and not tight to ensure consistency and ease of use.

Anatomy of a Stitch

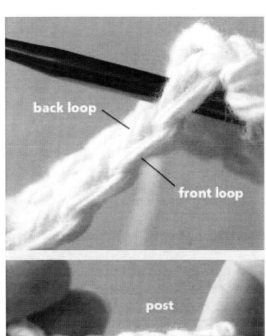

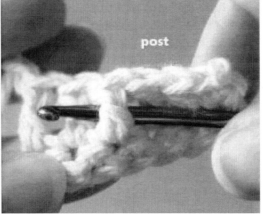

Crocheting into a Stitch

Unless specified otherwise, you will insert your hook under both loops to crochet any stitch.

Crocheting into the Front or Back of a Stitch

At times you will be instructed to crochet into the front loop only (flo) or the back loop only (blo) of a stitch to create a texture within the pattern.

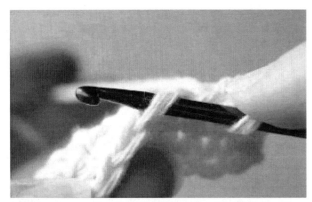

Inserting hook to crochet into the front loop only (flo) of a stitch.

Inserting hook to crochet into the back loop only (blo) of a stitch.

Slip Stitch (sl st)

The slip stitch is used to join one stitch to another or to join a stitch to another point.

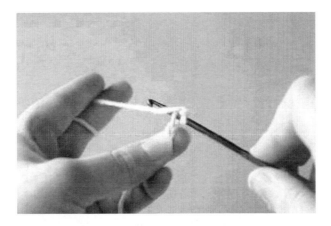

1. Insert the hook from the front of the stitch to the back of stitch and yarn over, just as for a chain stitch.

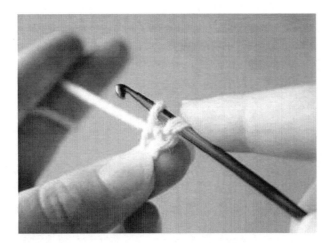

2. Pull the yarn back through the stitch: 2 loops on hook.

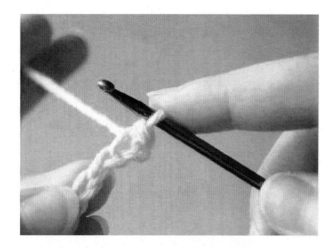

3. Continue to pull the loop through the first loop on the hook to finish.

Single Crochet (sc)

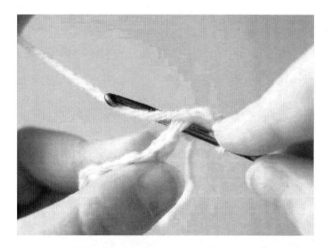

1. Insert the hook from the front of the stitch to the back and yarn over.

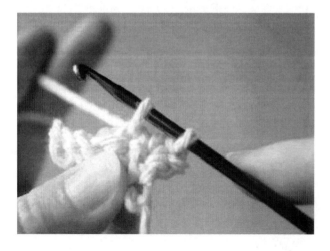

2. Pull the yarn back through the stitch: 2 loops on hook.

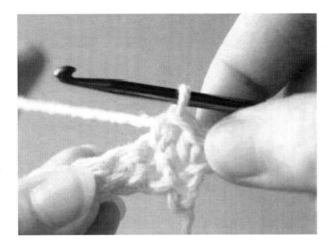

3. Yarn over and draw through both loops on the hook to complete.

Single Crochet Decrease (sc dec)

A single crochet decrease will take two stitches and make them into one single crochet stitch.

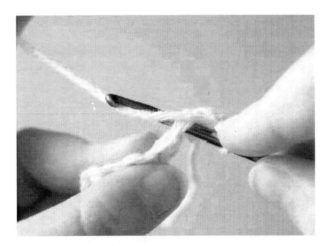

1. Insert the hook from the front of the stitch to the back and yarn over.

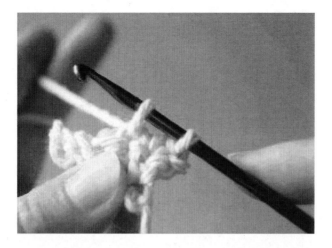

2. Pull the yarn back through the stitch: 2 loops on hook.

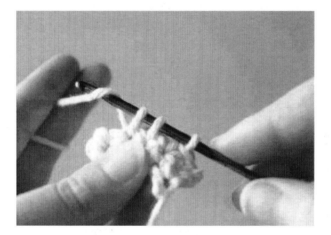

3. Leaving the loops on the hook, insert the hook front to back into the next stitch. Yarn over and pull back through stitch: 3 loops on hook.

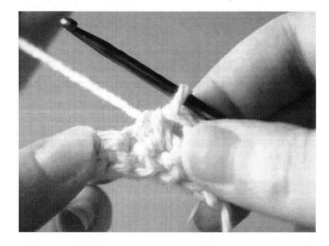

4. Yarn over and draw through all 3 loops on the hook to complete.

Half Double Crochet (hdc)

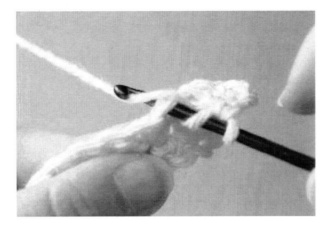

1. Yarn over and insert the hook from the front of the stitch to the back.

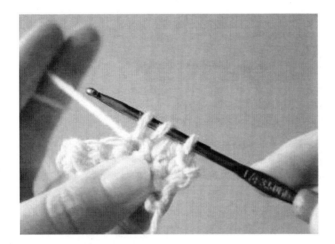

2. Yarn over and pull yarn back through stitch: 3 loops on hook.

3. Yarn over and draw through all 3 loops on hook to complete.

Half Double Crochet Decrease (hdc dec)

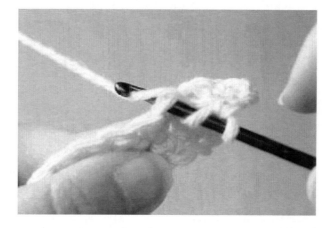

1. Yarn over and insert the hook from the front of the stitch to the back.

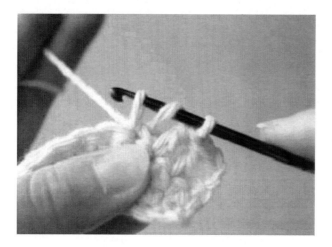

2. Yarn over and pull yarn back through stitch: 3 loops on hook.

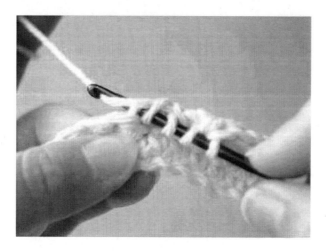

3. Yarn over and insert hook front to back into the next stitch.

4. Yarn over and pull yarn back through stitch: 5 loops on hook.

5. Yarn over and pull yarn through all 5 loops on hook to complete.

Double Crochet (dc)

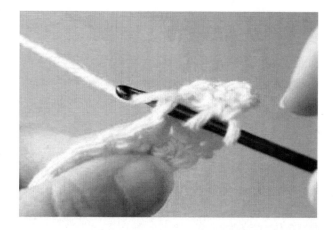

1. Yarn over and insert the hook from the front of the stitch to the back.

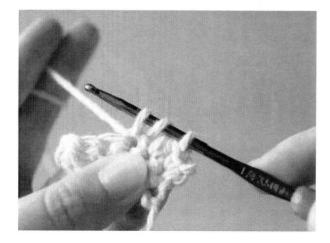

2. Yarn over and pull the yarn back through the stitch: 3 loops on hook.

3. Yarn over and draw the yarn through the first 2 loops on the hook: 2 loops on

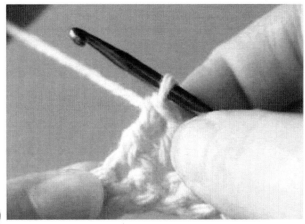

hook. (continued)

4. Yarn over and draw the yarn through the last 2 loops on hook to complete.

Double Crochet Decrease (dc dec)

A double crochet decrease will take two stitches and make them into one double crochet stitch.

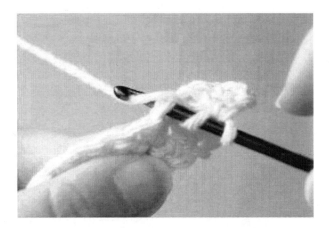

1. Yarn over and insert the hook from the front of the stitch to the back.

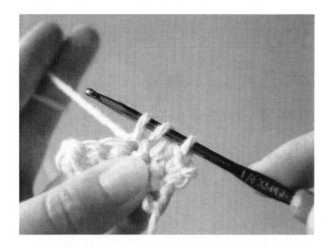

2. Yarn over and pull the yarn back through the stitch: 3 loops on hook.

3. Yarn over and draw the yarn through the first 2 loops on the hook: 2 loops on hook.

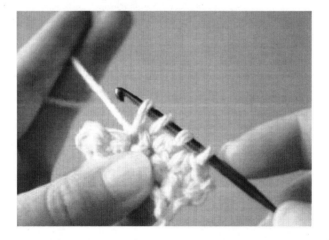

4. Leaving the loops on the hook, insert the hook front to back into the next

stitch. Yarn over and pull back through the stitch: 4 loops on hook.

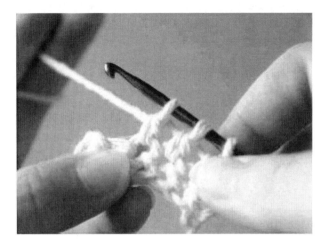

5. Yarn over and draw the yarn through the first 2 loops on the hook: 3 loops on hook.

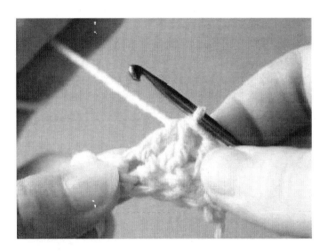

6. Yarn over and draw the yarn through all 3 loops on hook to complete.

Front Post Double Crochet (fpdc)

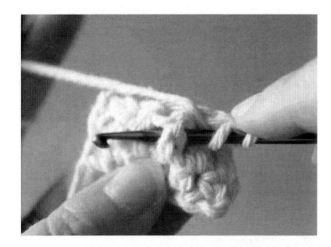

1. Yarn over and insert the hook from the front to the back to the front of the stitch around the post (see Anatomy of a Stitch on page 107 for where the post is located).

2. Yarn over and pull the yarn back around the post: 3 loops on hook.

3. Yarn over and draw the yarn through the first 2 loops on the hook: 2 loops on hook.

4. Yarn over and draw the yarn through last 2 loops on hook to complete.

Back Post Double Crochet (fpdc)

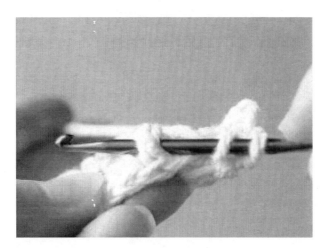

1. Yarn over and insert the hook from the back to the front to the back of the stitch around the post (see Anatomy of a Stitch on <u>page 107</u> for where the post is located). The photo shows the back of the stitch.

2. Yarn over and pull the yarn back around the post: 3 loops on hook.

3. Yarn over and draw the yarn through the first 2 loops on hook: 2 loops on hook.

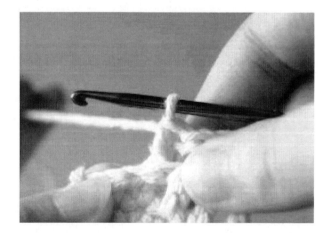

4. Yarn over and draw the yarn through last 2 loops on hook to complete.

Treble Crochet (tr)

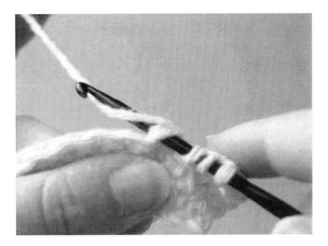

1. Yarn over 2 times and insert the hook from the front of the stitch to the back.

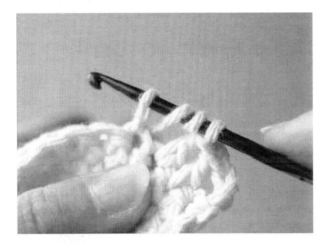

2. Yarn over and pull the yarn back through the stitch: 4 loops on hook.

3. Yarn over and draw the yarn through the first 2 loops on the hook: 3 loops on hook.

4. Yarn over and draw the yarn through the next 2 loops on the hook: 2 loops on hook.

5. Yarn over and draw the yarn through the last 2 loops on hook to complete.

Changing Colors

When switching yarns in a piece, use this technique for a clean color change.

1. Insert the hook through the next stitch and pull the yarn back through the stitch.

2. Yarn over with the NEXT color and pull through. The color change is complete. Cut the yarn for the original color.

If you are working a color change for a half double crochet, double crochet, or triple crochet, complete the stitch until the last pull through. Yarn over with the NEXT color and pull through to complete the color change.

Carrying Yarn

In patterns where you are switching back and forth between colors multiple times, you may be instructed to drop one yarn and pick up another instead of fastening off the original color. This is called carrying a yarn and it allows you to simply pick the yarn up later, with no ends to weave in. When you carry a yarn or yarns, it's very important to maintain an even tension when you pick up the carried yarn. If the yarn is carried too tightly, your fabric will pucker; if carried too loosely, the stitches can enlarge.

To carry a color, follow Steps 1 and 2 of Changing Colors on page 116. Do not cut the yarn when the color change is complete, but continue as directed here.

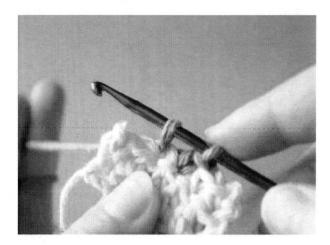

3. To change colors again, insert the hook through the next stitch and pull the yarn back through the stitch.

4. Drop the current color, yarn over with the color you are carrying, and pull through.

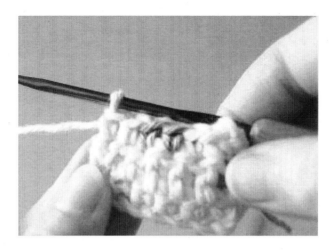

5. Repeat Steps 3 and 4 to carry.

Finishing Touches

Here we cover everything you need for a beautiful finish to your project, from seams to embellishments.

Fasten Off

When you reach the end of your crochet project, you will need to fasten off the yarn. To fasten off simply means to cut the yarn and secure the end. You will also need to fasten off one color to join another color within a project if you are working with multiple colors of yarn.

To fasten off, cut the yarn, leaving a few inches (unless otherwise instructed), and draw the yarn through the last loop on your hook.

Weave In Ends

1. Use your hook or a yarn needle to weave any cut ends up and down through 3 to 4 stitches. I also add a slip stitch to help secure the ends.

2. After weaving it, trim the end as close to the garment as possible to hide the end.

Fringe

It's so simple to add fringe to a hat or other garment for a bit of fun. You can follow these directions using any number of yarn strands cut to the same length and then folded in half together.

1. Insert the hook through the stitch where you wish the fringe to hang from the back of the stitch to the front, grab the center fold of the folded yarn strands, and pull through the stitch.

2. Pull the ends of the strands through the loops and pull tight.

Tassel

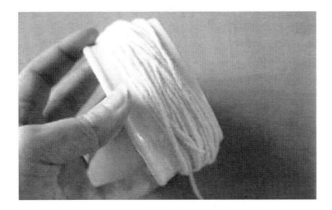

1. Wrap yarn around a large glass or piece of cardboard that is approximately 6" wide 40 times (or more, if you'd like the tassel to be thicker).

2. Carefully remove the yarn from the glass or cardboard. Hold the winding of yarn closed in one hand, tie a short length of yarn tightly around the hank about one-quarter of the way down on one end, and knot or slip knot it 2 to 3 times to secure.

3. Take another length of yarn and pull it through the loops of the short section of the hank. Tie it tightly and knot.

4. Cut the hank open at the long end and trim. Secure the tassel to the item by knotting the yarn from Step 3 securely.

Pom

1. Wrap yarn around a large glass or piece of cardboard that is approximately 6" wide 40 times (or more if you want the pom to be thicker).

2. Carefully remove the yarn from the glass or cardboard. Hold the winding of yarn closed in one hand, tie a short length of yarn tightly around the hank in the middle, and knot or slip knot it 2 or 3 times (shown in contrasting color).

3. Cut the hank open at each end and trim evenly. Secure the pom to the item by slipping a long piece of yarn through the yarn tied around the center and knotting to item securely.
4. Fluff the pom to finish.

Sewing Stitches

In many of these patterns, you will need to sew on an embellishment like a flower or eyes, or sew two pieces of a garment together, like the two halves of the Gily-Girl Poncho (page 67). Here are two stitches I often use, worked in a contrasting stitch so that 0ou can see how it is done.

Basic Sewing Stitch

Hold the right sides of the items together and, using your needle, go over and under both sets of stitches. Repeat.

This is what the stitches will look like (right sides facing out).

Whipstitch

1. Hold the right sides of the pieces together and go under the first 2 sets of

stitches. Do not go over the stitches.

2. Turn the hook and go back under the NEXT set of stitches. You will be working around the posts of the stitches.

3. Continue working around the posts of the stitches on either side.

As you whipstitch, notice that you're working around the posts and NOT over the stitches.

This is what the stitches will look like (right sides facing out).

Sewing Embellishments

When adding a crocheted piece (like a nose or eyes) to a hat or garment, simply sew it on with the yarn needle as shown.

1. Hold the piece on top of the garment and insert the yarn needle from the back to front using the last row of the piece to sew through.
2. Continue to sew around the piece until the edge is secure. Fasten off. Weave in ends.